A QUEST FOR TRUE ISLAM

A STUDY OF THE ISLAMIC RESURGENCE MOVEMENT AMONG THE YOUTH IN BANDUNG, INDONESIA

A QUEST FOR TRUE ISLAM

A STUDY OF THE ISLAMIC RESURGENCE MOVEMENT AMONG THE YOUTH IN BANDUNG, INDONESIA

Rifki Rosyad

Department of Archaeology and Anthropology
Faculty of Arts

February 1995

ANU
THE AUSTRALIAN NATIONAL UNIVERSITY

E PRESS

ANU
E PRESS

Published by ANU E Press
The Australian National University
Canberra ACT 0200, Australia
Email: anuepress@anu.edu.au
Web: http://epress.anu.edu.au

National Library of Australia
Cataloguing-in-Publication entry

      Rosyad, Rifiki.
      A quest for true Islam.

      Bibliography.
      ISBN 1 920942 32 7 (pbk.).
      ISBN 9781921313080 (web).

      1. Youth movement - Indonesia - Bandung. 2. Muslim youth -
      Indonesia - Bandung. 3. Muslim converts - Indonesia -
      Bandung. 4. Islam and politics - Indonesia - Bandung. 5.
      Islam and state - Indonesia - Bandung. I. Title.

      305.2308829757

Cover design by ANU E Press

Islam in Southeast Asia Series

Theses at The Australian National University are assessed by external examiners and students are expected to take into account the advice of their examiners before they submit to the University Library the final versions of their theses. For this series, this final version of the thesis has been used as the basis for publication, taking into account other changes that the author may have decided to undertake. In some cases, a few minor editorial revisions have made to the work. The acknowledgements in each of these publications provide information on the supervisors of the thesis and those who contributed to its development. For many of the authors in this series, English is a second language and their texts reflect an appropriate fluency.

Table of Contents

Foreword

A Quest for True Islam is a study of one of the most important movements of renewal in the history of Indonesian Islam. This movement began in the 1970s at a time when the Islamic world was entering its 15th century. It took shape in the 1980s and, in the late 1990s, developed a political dimension that has continued to carry forward efforts to the present.

A particular value of this study by Drs Rifki Rosyad derives from the fact that it was carried out, in the early 1990s, in the midst of the movement, when its various directions were by no means evident. Drs Rosyad saw the importance of the movement as a vital form of renewal and recognized its broad foundation among the Muslim student population of Indonesia. He was able to identify its beginnings at the Bandung Institute of Technology (ITB) and to chart its rapid spread and development in other universities throughout Indonesia.

The publication of this volume thus offers to a wider community a study of considerable research prescience. Drs Rosyad has done more than document the events of the period; he has captured the 'flavour' of the early 1990s with its defiant optimism amid frustration. He also provides an historical context for these occurrences and, importantly, links them to wider developments in the Islamic world.

As Drs Rosyad argues, no single factor can be cited as the cause of the Islamic resurgence that emerged in Bandung. A confluence of factors was of significance. To provide an understanding of these factors, Drs Rosyad examines the understanding of the contemporary situation and of a perceived history held by the key figures in the movement. This becomes an anthropology of the period in its relationship to the past.

A core segment of this study is based on interviews with activists, including M. Imaduddin Abdulrahim, associated with the Salman Mosque on the ITB campus. Although this study focuses on the inspiration provided by activities at the Salman Mosque, its strength is in its examination of what Drs Rosyad calls the 'fertile milieu' of the period that allowed a plethora of movements (*harakah*) to flourish, ranging from those of the *Ikhwan al-Muslimin, Hizb al Tahrir, Salafiyah, Dar al-Arqam*, or *Jama'ah Tabligh* to the efforts of the younger generational proponents of *Darul Islam*. Anyone interested in the current activities of these groups in Indonesia today would be well advised to read this study to appreciate the context of their inception. This is a perceptive and original research effort that offers many valuable insights.

Drs Rifki Rosyad was enrolled at The Australian National University as a student for two years from 1993 to 1995. As part of his study for the Masters degree, he conducted his research in Indonesia for his thesis. Since 1992, he has held the position of professor at the State Islamic University — Universitas Islam Negeri, UIN — Sunan Gunung Djati — Bandung and has continued to pursue a variety of research interests. It is important that his work be recognized among a wider audience for whom electronic publication represents the future.

James J. Fox

Acknowledgements

I would like to thank briefly all those who have been instrumental in making this thesis possible. I am particularly grateful to Professor James J. Fox for his supervision of this work, his continuous encouragement and the generous guidance and assistance I received from him throughout my studies at the Australian National University. His great interest in the anthropological study of Islamic community and culture -shown especially during my first year at the ANU- was significant in shaping my study. I am heavily indebted to Patrick Guinness, my co-supervisor, for, without his scholarly advice and comments, this study would not have appeared in its present form. Although the final form of this thesis has greatly benefitted from their help, I alone am responsible for its contents as well as its shortcomings.

I am also grateful to the Australian International Development Assistance Bureau (AIDAB) for its generous financial support without which the study could not have been carried out. My thanks also to all AIDAB officials, especially to Alicia Curtis for her assistance and attention during my study in Australia.

Profound thanks are due to those individuals in Bandung, including *ulama* and *mubaligh*, Muslim intellectuals and young Muslim activists, for their willingness to share with me what they knew, thought and felt about Islam and Muslim life in Indonesia. They are too many to be mentioned individually. Finally, I would like to acknowledge the help of my wife and children who assisted my work in various ways. They encouraged me by frequently asking *"Kapan Abi pulang?"*.

Abstract

This study attempts to present the contemporary Islamic resurgence movement among young people in Bandung Indonesia, focusing on its emergence, development and its routinisation. It traces various factors and conditions that contributed to the emergence of the movement. It also tries to explain how and why young people (students in particular) turn to Islam, and how the movement is organised and developed among students. Finally, it examines internal changes among various Islamic groups as responses to social, political and cultural changes.

The study indicates that this current Islamic resurgence is a continuation of a long-standing *tajdid* (renewal) tradition in Islam. Like previous Islamic renewal movements in Java, such as Muhammadiyah and PERSIS, it is an internal Muslim transformation in response to spiritual, social, political and cultural problems faced by Muslims. It is an attempt to maintain the Muslim commitment to the fundamental principles of Islam and to reconstruct an Islamic society in accord with the Qur'an and the *sunna*. The *tajdid* movement has always been two-fold: in spiritual terms it attempts to purge Islamic teachings and practices of non-Islamic influences and to present it once again in its original pure form; and in non-spiritual terms it is an endeavour to solve various problems faced by the Muslim community.

The difference between earlier Islamic movement and contemporary Islamic movements is that the current Islamic movements now occur in an era of globalisation, when the advance of electronic mass media has loosened national boundaries. This had several impacts on the current Islamic movement: first, international influence is not limited to Islamic ideas but also events; second, Islamic ideas can spread rapidly and widely regardless of national boundaries; third, one movement in one Muslim country can not only spread its ideas but can also establish its branches in other countries; finally, the growth of a global system reinforces the notion of a single Muslim community (*Ummah*).

Islamic resurgence is a global phenomenon throughout the Muslim world; however, it takes forms unique to each culture. Different from Islamic resurgence in the Middle East, Islamic resurgence in Indonesia has not been manifested in radical political activism and revolutionary actions. There was a tendency toward political revolutionary activism, but it carried little power. The common tendency rather is more cultural in its nature, i.e. to make Islam an ethical, moral and cultural foundation and to colour and fill the established social and cultural edifice with Islamic spiritual and moral content. This study propounds an understanding of the pattern in religious movements in the Islamic community and in Islamic cultures.

Chapter 1: Islamic Resurgence in Indonesia, an Introduction

1.1 The Moral Force: Bandung in Historical Perspective

Bandung, the capital of West Java, is a city with a long association with the structures of a modern industrialised nation. When the activities of the Dutch colonial government in this area increased in the late nineteenth century, central administrative offices, post office, telegraph and railroad system were established in Bandung. Bandung became an educational center for native islanders in the colonial period with the opening of a technical institute for indigenous students. Today it is called Bandung Institute of Technology (ITB), one of the most prestigious universities in Indonesia. In this university, Soekarno, the first president of Indonesia, finished his higher education, and in this university he established a study group, which became the forerunner of the Indonesian National Party (*PNI, Partai Nasional Indonesia*). In 1955 the city's importance in the Indonesian state was demonstrated symbolically, when it became a site of the Asia-Africa Conference of Non-aligned Nations.

In the Islamic history of Indonesia, Bandung was known as one of the most important places where a reformist and puritan Islamic organisation was established. In 1923, a group of merchants established an organisation called *Persatuan Islam* (*PERSIS*, Islamic Union). It was known because of its strict attitude to some Muslim customs, which were considered as superstition in contradiction with the main Islamic teachings (*aqidah*, faith), although other Muslims accepted those customs as proper Islam. It also accused the nationalist circle of wanting to establish Hindu and animism beliefs (Noer, 1987:13). The PERSIS's methods in promoting their ideas were very strong and even rough; members of the organisation often challenged and invited people to debate. Ideas of this organisation spread not only in Indonesia but also in Malaysia and Singapore. Among Indonesian intellectuals, *Persatuan Islam* ideas were spread through the writings and activities of Mohammad Natsir, a student of Ahmad Hasan, who was also the leader of *Masyumi* (*Majlis Syuro Muslimin Indonesia*, Consultative Council of Indonesian Muslim).[1]

Like Yogyakarta or Jakarta, Bandung is also known as a student city, in which two large universities ie. Bandung Institute of Technology and Padjadjaran

---

[1] *Masyumi* was a national Muslim organisation established during the Japanese occupation. At a National Islamic Meeting (*Muktamar Islam Indonesia*) held between 7–8 November 1945 in Yogyakarta, this organisation changed itself into an Islamic party. Most of Islamic organisations were represented within this party, but in 1952 *Nahdlatul Ulama* (*NU*, the Rise of the Religious Scholars), a conservative Islamic organisation, withdrew and became another Islamic party. In the 1955 election, *Masyumi* proved itself as the strongest party in the outer islands and in the West Java, while NU had the strongest support in East Java province.

University are located. These two universities are regarded as two of the nine universities of excellence in Indonesia (Railon:1985:23). Besides these universities, there are more than forty other higher education institutions, including private and public academies, institutes, and universities. Not surprisingly, students and lecturers from other places came to this city, and this situation has made Bandung a cosmopolitan city where the local Sundanese traditions are gradually adapted. The activities of these intellectuals made Bandung's intellectual, cultural and art life much more prominent (*Ibid,*:24).

Bandung is also a military centre. It is a center of the Sixth Regional Military Command (*KODAM, Komando Daerah militer VI*) Siliwangi, which for a long time has been regarded as one of the most professional of the Indonesian army ground forces (*Angkatan Darat*) with the best weaponry system. In Bandung are also located various military and police schools. Two of the most important institutions are the command staff college of the army ground forces (*SESKOAD, Sekolah Staf Komando Angkatan Darat*) and the joint command staff college of the army forces (*SESKOGAB, Sekolah Staf Komando Gabungan*). Besides these military schools, Bandung has several army groups scattered throughout the Bandung area.

Geographically, Bandung is very close to the national capital, Jakarta, only three or four hours' trip by bus or train from Jakarta. Elite from Jakarta usually come to Bandung and spend their weekend looking for fresh and cool air and a quiet environment. Likewise, many Bandung residents work in Jakarta, and every weekend they return to Bandung. This close relation creates an easy and smooth exchange of people and ideas between these two cities. International and national information is disseminated in Bandung at almost the same time as in Jakarta, and what happens in Bandung can immediately be heard in Jakarta.

Before the establishment of the New Order (*Orde Baru*) in 1965–66, Bandung became a place where the anti-Soekarno forces had wide support not only from the strictly Islamic groups, but also from student movements and military groups. Various events in early 1966 demonstrated Bandung students' important roles. They were always much braver and more radical than their colleagues in Jakarta. Although various important events took place in Jakarta , the role of Bandung's students was significant in decision making in Jakarta. Rahman Tolleng, the ex-chief editor of *Mahasiswa Indonesia*,[2] remarked "In Jakarta there might be a revolution, but Bandung is always the trigger".[3] Moreover, many political, social and art ideas are created or tested in Bandung before they are applied in Jakarta.

---

[2] *Mahasiswa Indonesia* (Indonesian Student), was a weekly student tabloid which played an important role in the establishment of the New Order. Through this publication student movements in Bandung spread their vision and analyses about the current situation of society. Besides, it became a means through which they expressed and unified opinion among those students organisations included in Indonesian Student United Action (*KAMI, Kesatuan Aksi Mahasiswa Indonesia*).

[3] Interview with an Economic Lecturer at the Indonesian University (UI) Jakarta, 3 November 1994.

Arief Budiman, as cited by Raillon (*Ibid,*:26), points out, "There is a tradition in Jakarta, that if we are dissappointed with the students' behaviour in Jakarta, we always turn to Bandung". Bandung became a city that complemented the national capital, Jakarta as "the political force" and Bandung as the "moral force". Budiman further says:

> With 'moral', it should be understood that they struggled based on right and wrong, just and unjust principles without considering political power. Whereas 'political force' means that student movements based their struggle on fertilising power, so that they were forced to political opportunism... Bandung ['s students] also have a peculiarity in their struggle, ie. their originality, and this is a manifestation of their creativity (*Ibid,*:26).

In the 1970s, Bandung became a center of attention not only at the national but also at the international level,[4] when student Islamic activities at Salman Mosque of ITB developed rapidly and provided a model of Islamic activities in university campuses throughout Indonesia.

1.2 Islamic Resurgence and Tajdid (Renewal) Tradition

In November 1979 Muslims throughout the world celebrated the beginning of the 15th century of Islamic calender (*hijriah*), which was expected as 'the century of Islamic Resurgence' (*Abad Kebangkitan Islam*). It was expected that by entering the new century, "Muslims would return to Islam, a religion and a way of life which is believed would increase Muslims' prestige and humanity" (Hamka and Saimima, 1980:1). In the 1970s in Muslim countries throughout the world, various social and political events occurred. These events included the application of Islamic law in Pakistan and Libya, the Islamic opposition movements in Egypt and Turkey, Muslim rebellions against Marxist government and Soviet invasion in Afganistan, and the Islamic separatist movement in Mindanao Island in the Philippines. Similar phenomena also occurred in Algeria, Tunisia, Sudan, Morocco, Malaysia and other countries where Muslims constituted the majority of the population. One of the most important events was the Iranian Revolution in 1979, which has influenced Islamic activists throughout the world.

Besides this political activism, there is a growing consciousness of Muslims toward Islam both in social and individual lives. In social life, this can be seen in the establishment of various Islamic institutions such as Islamic banks, organisations, laws, social welfare services and educational institutions. Likewise, in individual life, this can be seen in the increasing attention to religious observances such as mosque attendance, prayer, and Islamic dress, and from the

---

[4] Various reports on students Islamic activities at Salman can be found for instance in *New York Times*, 3 June 1979 page 3., Naipaul's travel diary *Among the Believers*, and in *Far Eastern Economic Review*, "An Islamic Revival threatens government moves to secularise the state," 24 January 1985.

increasing Islamic proselytization (*dakwah*). These political, social and individual manifestations of the Islamic resurgence can be seen throughout the Muslim world, in a variety of political, social and cultural settings.

In Indonesia such phenomena could also be seen in the mid-1970s when Islamic resurgence among young Muslim generations emerged. This was marked by the involvement of young people in various religious activities. Many young people went to the mosque where they learnt and discussed Islam. Such activities not only could be seen in various public mosques but also in school and university campuses. Moreover, many female students, both in senior high schools and universities started to wear the veil (*kerudung*).[5] This was followed by the emergence of various *Ikatan Remaja Masjid* (Youth Mosque Associations) in public mosques and Islamic preaching institutions in university campuses (Lembaga Dakwah Kampus). In every large public mosque (*Majid Jami* or *Masjid Raya*) there was always a youth sector, which organised Islamic activities for youth. *Istiqamah* Mosque in Bandung, *Sunda Kalapa* and *Al-Azhar* Mosques in Jakarta figured prominently in these activities. In almost every university there was an institution which organised Islamic activities. From these universities the *da'wah* movement spread gradually to other surounding universities. The spread of the movement took place through mutual campus visitation, Islamic preaching institutions, and coordinated joint activities.

In the 1980s there was another phenomenon, namely the emergence and development of various Islamic movements, known as *Harakah* (an Arabic, 'movement'). Different from conventional and formal Islamic movements, such as Muhammadiyah, Nahdlatul Ulama or Persatuan Islam (Persis), these Islamic movements were not formal Islamic organisations, and some of them were even called underground movements. Moreover, unlike those formal Islamic movements founded by great ulama, the experts in traditional Islamic knowledge, these new Islamic movements were founded and pioneered by young *mubaligh* (preachers), most of them not trained in the traditional Islamic education system, *pesantren*, but in public schools and universities. The main base of these movements was usually the various campus Islamic preaching institutions (*LDK, Lembaga Dakwah Kampus*) and the public mosques.

Like Islamic movements in other parts of the world, there are three main themes of this new Islamic phenomenon, namely: the application of Islamic law (*shariah*), making Islam a way of life, and the freedom from non-Muslim political and cultural domination. Politically and sociologically, these themes derived from the awareness that the Islamic community (*Umat Islam*), even when in a majority, was internally politically, economically and religiously weak. Religiously, these

---

[5] They knew that they were not allowed by their schools and universities to do so. As a result, some of them moved to Islamic private schools. This is because Department of Education's acts forbade students to wear something on the head.

themes derived from a belief that Muslims have departed from true Islamic values due to the infiltration and assimilation of both local indigenous and foreign un-Islamic beliefs and practicies. The political and economic life of the Islamic community, in their view, has for a long time been controlled by other religious and ethnic minority groups. Moreover, they also assert that Islam, as the religion of the majority, has not been able to inspire the social and cultural life of the Indonesian community. Two intellectual Muslims explained:

> The development of communication technology has been controlled by 'other people', who forced us to neglect religion (Islam) in our lives. Every night television programs, which entered our bed rooms, tempted us to leave Islamic values. Moreover, reading sources in our homes, such as books, magazines and newspapers are almost all provided by those who ruin our faith and belief (*Iman* and *Aqidah*). As a result of this, areas formerly regarded as Islamic regions, such as the 'Mecca veranda' (*Serambi Mekkah*)[6] and other places, are now penetrated by "modern" culture with its all lousiness (*kebrengsekannya*), prostitution, gambling and other wickednesses, which are regarded as proper things…

> It is clear that politically from the old order till the new order, the Islamic community, although they are a majority in this country, has always been cornered (*terpojok*) (Hamka and Saimima 1979:3).

 Through religious legitimation, these new Islamic movements tried to transform their present societies into the ideal society exemplified by the Prophet Muhammad. To achieve this, like many previous Islamic revival movements, they encouraged Muslims to return to the Qur'an and the Sunnah (model and example) of the Prophet. Based on these prime sources, they believed that Islam is the only solution of those problems faced by Muslims. For them, Islam is a total way of life which is applicable to all times and places. There is no separation between the religious and worldly life, and between state and religion. The main goal of these movements is the government of a community based on the God's revealed law (*Sharia*). Within this ideal community, God is sovereign over all people, and individual freedom is guaranteed. Those who resist this goal, either Muslims or non-Muslims, are regarded as enemies of God.

This research is concerned with these phenomena of the Islamic resurgence movement among young people in Bandung, focusing on its emergence, development and routinisation, which took place between the 1970s and the early 1990s. The subject I have studied, borrowing Nakamura's[7] term, is an "on going [process] of Islamisation … in which a substantial number of Muslims regard prevailing religious situations (often including themselves) as

---

[6] *Serambi Mekah* is another name of Aceh, it refers to a place which has strong Islamic bases.

[7] Mitsuo Nakamura is a professor of Anthropology at Chiba University Japan. He has written book and papers on Islam in Indonesia including *The Crescent Arises over the Banyan Tree*.

unsatisfactory and, as a corrective measure, strive to live up to what they conceived as the standard of the orthodox teaching of Islam" (1983:2). Such a process, Nakamura further said, is a "self-conscious re-Islamisation of Muslims by themselves... [which] emphasized not only the necessity to conform to the ritual orthodoxy of Islam but also the genuine devotion to fulfilling the moral and ethical teaching of Islam" (*Ibid*).

Contemporary Islamic resurgence in Indonesia, like Islamic movements in other parts of the Islamic world is deeply rooted in the Muslim medieval and modern historical experience. Muslim historical heritage provides bases, symbols and concepts for the current Islamic resurgence. Contemporary Islamic resurgence, like previous Islamic movements, is a reflection of longstanding tradition and continuation of a renewal (*tajdid*) tradition in Islamic history (Voll, 1983:32–47 and Ahmad, 1983:222). It is an expression of the revitalization of Islamic faith and practices as an attempt to bring Muslim individual and communal life into the right path based on the Qur'an and *Sunnah*. Besides this notion of *tajdid*, there is also the Islamic idea of *dakwa* (to call people, especially Muslims to obey the divine command and to model the life of the Prophet Muhammad) and of *al-amru bi al-makruf wa al-nahy an al-munkar* (to command the good and forbid the evil) which obliges every Muslim individual to correct any kind of impurity and corruption within society.

The notion of *tajdid* (renewal) in the Islamic tradition can be traced back to the Prophet Muhammad, who said that "At the turn of each century there will arise in this *ummah* (the Muslim community) these who will call for a religious renewal (revival)".[8] Such people (*mujaddid*),[9] are believed to always come in the time when Muslim community departs from the true path defined by the Qur'an and *sunnah* (example of the Prophet). The task of the *mujaddid*, therefore, is to return Muslims to their basic sources (the Qur'an and *sunnah*), to clean Islam from all un-Godly elements, to present Islam and make it flourish more or less in its original pure form and spirit (Maududi, 1981:34–5 and Voll, 1983:).

The source of validity of this Islamic renewal (*tajdid*) is the perfect model available in the revelation, Qur'an (*wahyu*, words of God) and the traditions and customs of the Prophet (*sunnah*). The era of the Prophet is an ideal model of a society in which revelation is applied in human life. The purpose of the *tajdid* is to implement this ideal model in Muslims' lives, wherever and whenever Muslim society exists. This purpose implies that *tajdid* is a continuous effort by Muslims always to explain Islam and make it applicable in continually changing situations without violating its principles. Contemporary Islamic resurgence, therefore, is inspired by the example of past experience, not by a hope for a future utopia

---

[8] This quotation related by Abu Huraira in *Sunan* (a collection of *Hadits*, traditions of the Prophet) of Abu Dawud (Cairo 1348 Hijri)
[9] The activity of renewal is *tajdid*, and the person who brings it about is called a *mujaddid*.

like messianic or millenarian movements, which depend on the notion of the future when a saviour or Messiah will appear. Nevertheless, the *tajdid* tradition in Islam cannot be seen as conservatism[10] because of its past orientation. This is because, as history has shown,*tajdid* movements often criticise the established institutions and traditions, and even by revolution challenge the existing system. Moreover, the progressive ideas of the *tajdid* tradition and current Islamic resurgence are demonstrated in their basic acceptance and accommodation to modernity[11] (Cantory 1990:183–94). The notion of the ideal era of the past here should be understood as a perennial model and not as antiquated custom.

The difference between contemporary *tajdid* (renewal) and the previous ones is that the contemporary *tajdid* movement occurs in an era of globalisation in which the electronic revolution in mass communication has broken down boundaries between countries. Satellites, transmitters and television networks make the citizens of the world a global community. In such a situation the insistence on Muslim unity in a single Islamic international community (*Ummah*) becomes a reality. The growth of global systems of communication, according to Bryan S. Turner (1994:90), "[reinforced] the concept of Islam as a global system." Such a situation also influenced the way *tajdid* ideas and movements have emerged and spread. Through global communication systems *tajdid* ideas and movements in one Muslim country can rapidly spread to other Muslim countries. This makes it possible for one movement in a Muslim country to have branches in other Muslim countries, a phenomenon that never existed before.

1.3 Islamic Resurgence: a Definition

Different observers have named these new phenomena Islamic revivalism, revitalisation, upsurge, reassertion, renewal, awakening. Others have called these phenomena Islamic fundamentalism, neo-fundamentalism, militant Islam, and political Islam. All these names are useful to analyse the new wave of Islamic movements, but they cover only certain aspects of the phenomena and neglect others.

---

[10] According to Charlotte Seymour-Smith (1986:53), conservatism is "the preference and maintenance of traditional ways of acting, forms of social institutions and cultural patterns."

[11] Their acceptance of modernity can be seen in their adoption of modern institutions and technology. Many of the leaders of Islamic movements are graduates of major universities from faculties of medicine, science and engineering: some of them are even graduates from Western universities.*Ulama* and Muslim activists harnessed modern technology to organise and mobilise mass support as well as disseminate their religious messages and their socio-political activism. The wide-spread use of mass communication technology such as radio, television and video-cassettes, computers and fax machines established effective communication among these activists. What they reject from the modernity is that, as Esposito (1992:11) points out, "secularisation is a sine qua non for modernisation." Moreover, since the notion of modernisation -often equated with the idea of development- was Western in its origin and form, when it is applied in the Muslim world it inevitably leads to"occidentalisation" or "Westernisation" (cf. Sardar 1977:39). They selectively accept some aspects of modernity and reject what they believed is non-Islamic.

'Islamic reassertion', the term used by Mohammed Ayoob (1981), for example, captures the idea of regaining power and position by the Islamic movements, but it does not reflect the notion of threat and challenge to the *status quo* and the dominant paradigms (Muzaffar 1987). Moreover, it merely conveys the political aspects of the Islamic movement, but neglects other aspects of the movements, such as social and ritual aspects, which are the main characteristics of these movements as religious movements.

Similarly, the 'Islamic revivalism' concept does capture the idea of idealising the era of the Prophet and his companions. It suggests the notion of reviving practices and ideas and the notion of renaissance and renewal of thought. This is a true description of certain segments of the Islamic movements, but it does not explain their whole outlook. The notion of back to the Qur'an and the *Sunnah* (the example and tradition of the Prophet) and idealising the period of the Prophet and his companions, does not mean going back 1500 years to antiquated traditions and practices. 'Back to Qur'an and *Sunnah*' means reinforcing Muslims' loyalty to 'perennial and eternal values' (Muzaffar, 1987:3).

Likewise 'Islamic Fundamentalism', the most common term used by Western press and even academics, merely explains minor aspects of the current Islamic phenomena. To quote Esposito (1992:7) the term 'Islamic Fundamentalism' "tells us everything and yet, at the same time, nothing". It is true that Islamic movements call Muslims to return to their basic fundamental faith and beliefs (*Aqidah*). However, the word 'fundamentalism', which derives from a unique phenomenon in a certain period of American Protestanism, is not appropriate to the current phenomena in Islam (cf. Khurshid Ahmad, 1987:226). 'Fundamentalist' in Christian traditions refers to those "who advocate a literalist biblical position and is thus regarded as static, retrogressive and extremist... and wish to return to and replicate the past" (Esposito 1992:7). In fact leaders and founders of the so-called 'Islamic Fundamentalist movement', are Western educated people,[12] and are fond of modern technology. In addition, the image of 'Islamic Fundamentalism' as "political activism, extremism, terrorism, fanatism and anti-Americanism" might be true to refer to some radical religiopolitical activism, especially in the Middle East. Many Islamic movements, however, are involved within the existing system. Furthermore, as Gregory F. Rose, an Assistant Professor at the University of North Texas observes (1990:219–28), the main problem with the term 'fundamentalism' is a not semantic one, but a 'misconceptualization' as a result of misleading cross-cultural analogies.[13]

---

[12] Many of them even are Western educated, or at least they studied Western knowledge. Sayyid Qutb, an important thinker of *Ikhwan al-Muslimin* (Muslim Brotherhood) movement in Egypt, Imam Khomeini, the Iranian spiritual leader, studied and lived respectively in the United States and France

[13] Rose (1990:220) argues that although the notion of fundamentalism was first applied to nineteenth-century American religious movements, the term was later colored by Talcott Parson, in his study of the 'fundamentalism reaction' (his analyses of the rise of European Fascist movements. Rose recognises that Parson regarded fundamentalist reaction as a "pathological, authoritarian reconstruction

'Fundamentalism', he argues, is an "ethnocentric, militantly secularist sociological categorization", which in turn makes it difficult to analyse comprehensively the current Islamic resurgence.

Like many recent observers, such as Hillal Dessouki, Chandra Muzaffar, John Esposito and Daniel Regan,[14] I will use term the 'Islamic resurgence'. Borrowing Muzaffar's (1987) idea, the word resurgence, meaning "reappearance and growth of a particular attitude or activity among a group of people, especially one which has been forgotten for some time" (Collin Cobuild Dictionary 1992) perfectly explains the current emergence of new Islamic movements. In Muslims' view, Islam has been for a long time forgotten by Muslims themselves, and now they are increasingly aware of their Islamic identity. Through their attachment to Islam they regain their self esteem and dignity, and this indicates clearly that Islam has become important again in Muslims' lives. Another point is that the word "reappearance" explains the relation between the recent development of Islamic movements and the past glory of Islam and the ideal society in the era of Prophet and his companions. As Muzaffar (1987:2) puts it, the term resurgence represents the idea of challenge and threat. Many Muslims believe that Islam as an alternative way of life challenges the dominant social systems. On the other hand, the dominant groups and those who are being challenged, view their position as being threatened by these Islamic movements.

Two good definitions of Islamic resurgence have been offered by Khurshid Ahmad, Chandra Muzaffar and Hillal Dessouki. A combination of these definitions, I believe, are representative enough to explain current Islamic development throughout the world. According to Ahmad (1987:226), Islamic resurgence is a "future-oriented movement" concerned with the problems of modernity and the challenges of technology and offering solutions based on the original sources of Islam, the Qur'an and *Sunnah*. It is a movement that on the bases of these sources tries flexibly and capably to innovate what have been neglected by conservatives who stick to a particular school of *fiqh* (law).

Another definition offered by Muzaffar (1987:2) says that:

> Islamic resurgence is a description of the endeavour to re-establish Islamic values, Islamic practices, Islamic institutions, Islamic laws, indeed Islam in its entirety, in the lives of Muslims everywhere. It is an attempt to

of an idealized social *status quo ante* in response to increasingly high levels of dysfunction in the existing social *status quo*." In Parson's view, regardless of source, every challenge to the established social order is regarded as deviant, residual and marginal. Therefore, Rose concludes, treating religion as residual and marginal shows the uncritical acceptance of Parsonian functionalism and its assumptions, and the insistent belief that despite social disruption, a Western model of economic and political development could be applied comprehensively in non-Western settings.

[14] See respectively their books *Islamic Resurgence in The Arab World, Islamic Resurgence in Malaysia, Voices of Resugent Islam* and "Islamic Resurgence: Characteristics, Causes, Consequences and Implications", in *Journal of Political and Military Sociology*, 21. No 2. Winter 1993.

re-create an Islamic ethos, an Islamic social order, at the vortex of which is the Islamic human being, guided by the Qur'an and the Sunnah."

Dessouki (1982:4) defines 'Islamic resurgence' as referring to

"an increasing political activism in the name of Islam by governments and opposition groups alike. It designates a politicized, activist form of Islam and the growing use of Islamic symbolism and legitimation at the level of political action... We are not dealing with calls for or attempts to provide a new interpretation of the Qur'an but, rather, with social and political movements that are engaged in mobilization, organization and possibly the seizure of political authority. Thus [it] refers to the increasing prominence and politicization of Islamic ideologies and symbols in Muslim societies and in the public life of Muslim individuals"

When these definitions are attached to the word 'movement' they refer to a "worldwide, open and diffuse system in which individual Muslims or Muslims organised in groups are consciously working towards the reconsolidation of the Ummah into a behavioural, operational and goal seeking system" (Siddiqui, 1980:9). Based on these definitions the resurgent Islamic youth movement in Bandung Indonesia is a part of the worldwide Islamic movement which endeavours to establish Islamic values, practices, institutions, laws, politics and its entirety in Muslims' lives everywhere.

Chapter 2: The Foundation of the Movement

2.1 Introduction

Although they had in common, the growing attachment of Muslims to Islam, Islamic resurgences that occurred throughout the Muslim world from the 1970s, were historically and behaviorally diverse and complex phenomena (Dessouki 1982:6). In each Muslim country -even within each Muslim country- there were always different causes, different historical backgrounds and different cultural settings. In the Middle East, for example, Islamic resurgence often occurred through radical political activism, whereas in Malaysia and Indonesia it is manifested respectively through Malay ethnicity (Muzaffar 1985: 14–6) and through the Islamic cultural movement.

From a sociological point of view, it is difficult to pin-point one absolute cause of a social phenomenon. It comprises various factors which directly or indirectly affect one another. A social movement, for example, is an accumulation of various factors, including the emergence of radical ideological powers, class consciousness, group and race identity, nationality and the emergence of important (charismatic) figures, who are able to mobilise power. These factors are not sufficient for the emergence of a social movement, without a conducive social millieu and an apt social issue or event that triggers the movement. These may include leadership disintegration, social chaos, economic problems, national instability, and foreign influence and intervention (Perry and Perry 1988;280–2, cf. Tolkhah 1994:9).

Similarly, there is no single factor which caused the emergence of Islamic resurgence movement among young people in Bandung. To understand this phenomenon at least four important aspects should be considered: socio-historical backgrounds, radical ideology, foreign influence and individual personalities. In examining these I restrict myself to the history of student movements from the early period of the New Order, ie late 1965, to late 1979. This history is important because Islamic youth movements emerged, when the student movements seemed to be dead.

Secondly I analyse how the founders and their followers perceived the history of Islam in Indonesia, and how they viewed social and political situations at the time they initiated the movement. The study of perceptions of the past, as Gungwu puts it, "is an attempt to understand the contemporary values of some periods of the past … [which] constitutes a valuable background for explaining what is happening today" (1979:6). It is important to understand these historical perceptions since they can be adjusted along with radical changes of the world around, and can deliberately be used 'for social and political purposes' (1979:2).

Islam was understood by the founders and the followers of the movements as an alternative ideology and civilisation which completely contradicts other world ideologies such as socialism and capitalism. Such a view is very different from previous Islamic movements such Muhammadiyah, PERSIS (*Persatuan Islam*, The Unity of Islam) and NU (*Nahdlatul Ulama*, The Rise of Islamic Scholars) that put much more emphasis on ritual, social and political aspects.

My third interest is to examine to what extent international Islamic movements and foreign influences played a role in the emergence and development of Islamic youth resurgence movements in Indonesia.

Lastly the individual background of the founders is significant in understanding the movement. I will observe the background of only one of the founders, including his familial and educational background, and his relation to the emergence of the movement.

2.2 Student Movement and Political Suppression

Students' interest in social problems lead to their involvement in politics. Students, according to Curran and Renzetti (1990:598), "have a long history of activism in such political pressure groups". Such a position, in Lipset's view, is gained because students "are more responsive to political trends, to changes in mood, to opportunities for action, than almost any other group in the population" (Lipset and Altbach 1969:497). This shows that the role of students in society is not only as social critic, but also as a political force which can stimulate social and political change within society.

In developing countries, the role of students in society is very important because they are elite groups who are among the first introduced to modernisation. This was even clearer in the post-colonial era, between 1950s and 1970s, when very few people had access to higher education. Within a society with a small number of educated middle class, students became a source of public opinion. Moreover, their concern with modernisation and development made them important agents of social, political and cultural changes. They began to diverge from the traditional prescriptions to which the older generation was very much attached, instigating, as Feuer (1969) puts it, a "conflict of generations".

In Indonesia this conflict of generations was marked by various student demonstrations which criticised government policies and proposed radical changes and solutions to social, economical and political problems faced by Indonesia. In the 1960s students and other sections of society, including some army members (Railon 1985:7) struggled for the establishment of the Indonesian New Order. In the New Order era student movements continued to criticise government policies. In 1974 students demonstrations demanded the dissolution of the group of personal assistants of the president who had too much influence at the time, a reduction in prices and the crushing of the corruptors. This demonstration turned into violence and destruction when demonstrators' behaviour went out of control, and about 9 students were killed and 23 others were injured (*Tomtowi Syafei* 1987). This event was known as 'Peristiwa Malari' (The Fifteenth of January Event).

This event had a long and tragic impact on student activism. In 1977, the Ministry of Education banned student involvement in politics. It was followed by the dissolution of Student Government (*Dewan Mahasiswa, Dema*) in 1978, by order of the Pangkopkamtib (*Panglima Komando Pemulihan Keamanan dan Ketertiban*, the Chief of Operations Command for the Restoration of Security and Order), Admiral Sudomo. Finally, on April 19th 1978, the Ministry of Education decided on a new policy, ie. Normalisation of Campus (*Normalisasi Kehidupan Kampus, NKK*). A year later students protested against this policy in Bandung, Jakarta, Surabaya and Jogjakarta (CSIS 1980:15), but, the policy still applies in 1995.

For students, this was the death of university campuses. According to a student, the NKK policy resulted in disadvantages not only to the students but also to the government. Students became passive and were no longer interested in the social and political problems of their societies. They were alienated from their surrounding environment and frustrated. Their ideal intellectual and spiritual dimensions disappeared. They become bodies (*tubuh*) without soul (*ruh*). In MH Ainun Najib's view, students became bulls in the stall of NKK.

From 1983 Islamic student organisations such as HMI (*Himpunan Mahasiswa Islam*, Islamic Student Association), PMII (*Pergerakan Mahasiswa Islam Indonesia*, Indonesian Islamic Student Movement), IMM (*Ikatan Mahasiswa Muhammadiyah*, Muhammadiyah Student Association) and PII (*Pelajar Islam Indonesia*, Islamic School-Student Association),[1] were forced to change their ideological base, ie. Islam, into Pancasila. In the 15th HMI Congress inMedan, HMI decided not to adopt Pancasila as its *azas* (foundation), even though there was strong external pressure from the government. However, in 1985 when the government began to apply the Basic Guidelines for Mass Organisations (*Rancangan Undang-Undang Keormasan*), all mass organisations, including here students' and religious organisations were required to accept Pancasila as their bases. Therefore, in the 16th congress, after a long and heated debate HMI accepted Pancasila. This attitude led to internal conflict, ie. the break-up of HMI into HMI itself and the 'Assembly to save the organisation,' (*Majelis Penyelamat Organisasi, MPO*). Muhammadiyah Student Association (IMM) and Indonesian Islamic Student Movement (PMII) automatically accepted Pancasila when their main body Muhammadiyah and NU, respectively, accepted it as the foundation of all organisations. Only one organisation, the PII, preferred to dissolve itself rather

---

[1] In Indonesia there are two terms which refer to the word 'student'in English First students of High school and below are called *'pelajar.'* The other term is *'mahasiswa,'* which refers to students of higher education institution, universitiesand academies.

than accept Pancasila as its ideological foundation. Although it formally dissolved, it continued to hold trainings at an underground level.

This situation for Muslims and students in general was quite frustrating. To reduce their alienation they tried to find channels through which they could express their ideas. At this stage public and university mosques became a centre of student activities.

The late 1970s and early 1980s (after the banning of *Dewan Mahasiswa*), according to Denny J.A., (1990), marked a new stage in the student movement in Indonesia. Student movements changed their orientation, format, organisation and type. While the orientation of previous student movements was challenging the 'power structure' (*struktur kekuasaan*), in the 80s their orientationwas to form political and social opinion among the masses.

2.3 Historical Perception: Disappointment of The Past

In concentrating on this historical perception my intention is to relate the founders' perceptions of the past to their response to contemporary situations. These past perceptions contribute "a valuable background for explaining what is happening today, why contemporary [people]respond as they do to current developments and in what ways they are likely to interpret presentevents in the future" (Gungwu 1979:6).

In the view of the founders and followers of various Islamic youth movements, the history ofIslam in Indonesia is the history of "continuous defeat and dissappointment." [2] For them it is ironical that throughout history Indonesian Muslims have been the majority of the Indonesian population, but have always been marginal politically. Islamicparties and organisations have been impotent. The Indonesian government has actually been dominated by other powers. Although some Muslims have been involved in the government, Muslims have seen it as un-Islamic. In their view government has been infiltrated by Christians, and government policies identified with Christian policies directly or indirectly push Islam into a 'corner' (*terpojok*). [3] Since the birth of the New Order, Christian figures have occupied some very important and strategic positions in the country.

In the view of Muslim activists, the role of Muslims in the independence movement began since three centuries ago, with resistance movements against the Dutch by Muslim sultanates and leaders. Due to this continuous resistance by Muslims, Indonesia was increasingly identified with Islam, and the Dutch with Christianity, since Christianity was introduced with colonialism. The Dutch were seen as *kafir* (infidel) who not only wanted to control the country politically and economically but also to destroy Islam. This identification of the Dutch

---

[2] Interview with some of the founders of Islamic movements and many youth Muslim activists.
[3] The word *terpojok* (cornered, marginalised) was a common theme among the young Muslim activists to describe the position of Islam in Indonesia.

Christian as a threat and enemy of Islam became the roots of political conflict between Christians and Muslims in the period of post-independence, when the issue of Jakarta Charter (*Piagam Jakarta*)[4] emerged (Hasan 1980:7).

Most movements and revolts were crushed by the Dutch. However, the Dutch had to pay a high price in terms of money and human life. The resistance movement of the Acehnese was successfully crushed after Dr. Snouck Hurgronje, an Islamic specialist, studied Islam in Aceh.[5] His report on Aceh was then used to plan an effective strategy to surpass the Acehnese. He was appointed as the Dutch government specialist for Islamic affairs, and he developed an effective policy to prevent and destroy any forms of an Islamic resistance movement. His policies became more important when the Dutch realised that the biggest challenge to their domination was coming from *ulama* a and Islamic leaders. One of the most important policies of Snouck Hurgronje was to encourage Islamic religious activities (ritual aspects), while preventing and proscribing any attempts to develop a powerful Islamic political base. This policy, according to Muslim activists, continued to be applied by the Sukarno and Suharto regimes (cf. Samson 1972:229–30).

Indonesian history, for Muslims especially the militant, has been an irony. In the political sphere, throughout history, Indonesian Muslims, who are the majority of the Indonesian population, were characterised as 'outsiders' (McVey 1983:199–225). Indonesian Muslims have been characterised, borrowing Wertheim's (1980) term, as a "majority with [a] minority mentality". Indeed, as Drakeley (1992) puts it, throughout the New Order (Orde Baru) period Islam in Indonesia has occupied a position as political outsider, "despite being a crucial political midwife at its birth" (p.5).

Furthermore, Muslim activists believed that the Muslim *ummat* (community), organisationally and individually, was often sold out by both Muslim and non-Muslim leaders. Islamic power was always used and exploited, but it was neglected when the glory was gained (Rosidi 1970). One informant said, "When this country was in a crisis Muslims, who were the majority of the population, were always in the front line, but when the crisis was over the Muslims were ignored." This awareness led to a belief that there must be something wrong

---

[4] The Jakarta Charter (*Piagam Jakarta*) was a draft preamble of the Constitution of 1945 (*Undang-Undang Dasar 45*) which said that the state was "based on belief in God with the obligation for adherents of Islam to carry out Islamic law" ("*berdasar ketuhanan, dengan kewajiban menjalankan syariat Islam bagi pemeluk-pemeluknya*") (Boland 1985:28). According to Hasan (1980:8), this was a minimal demand from Muslims during the debate on the national state base in 1945. After heated debate between nationalist secularists, Christians and Muslims, the last seven words known as the "tujuh kata" (seven words) were finally dropped from the draft preamble because -it was believed-they would create religious conflict and in turn destroy national unity.

[5] It was reported that he studied Islam in Mecca and disguised himself as a Muslim. One of the important concepts is his three categories of Islam: as pure religion, social aspect and political aspect. For further information of Islamic Politics of Dutch Colonial Government see Husnul Aqib Suminto in his *Politik Islam Pemerintah Hindia Belanda*, especially between pages 115 to 125.

with the ummat. Among other things, Muslims realised that Islam was remote from the ummat. In a public sermon, one *mubaligh* (preacher) even said that the Quran had been treated as a house decoration. *Hadits* (the traditions of the Prophet) had been left behind.

Muslims have always been in opposition to the government not only because of Suharto, who ignored and suppressed Muslims' aspirations, but also because of the people surrounding him. Some big mass media, publishers and social infrastructures were controlled by Christian institutions. Furthermore, Christian missions which successfully converted Muslims in many parts of Indonesia, were regarded as a big challenge for Muslims. These facts, according to Mursalin Dahlan, one of the founders of Islamic resurgence in Bandung, "showed that Islam, as in the colonial era, has been dominated and controlled by other powers that were always hostile to Islam."

2.4 Islam: The Only Alternative

Basically, the core of Islamic teachings developed by the Islamic resurgence movement is similar to other Islamic groups. Their teachings are based on similar sources, ie. Quran and *Sunnah* (tradition of the Prophet). The differences are tied to the way they approach Islam. These differences result in various religious views, such as reformist, modernist, traditionalist, and fundamentalist (Aziz 1989:236).

According to one informant, Muslims' view of Islam was deeply influenced by Snouck Hurgronje, who tried to restrict Islam to a 'the mosque religion' (*agama mesjid*) and deny its social and political life (cf. Suminto 1985:122 and Samson 1972:229–30). Islam, in the view of young Muslim activists, for a long time has been misunderstood by Muslims, and because of this misunderstanding, Islam has been mocked and humiliated by other powers. Islam, in Mohammad Abduh's[6] term, "has been covered up by Muslims" (*al-Islamu mahjubun bi al-Muslimin*). I found there was a general dissatisfaction among important figures of the movement with the concept of Islam offered by previous ulama and mainstream Islam. Moreover, some ulama in the view of young Muslims were afraid to explain the 'true Islam'. Because of this, young activists preferred young and 'brave' preachers.

This new tendency was related to the wide distribution of Islamic translations. Almost all reference books of the movements came from the Middle East, and other Muslim countrries. Some of those important books were written by Sayyid Qutb, Hasan al-Banna and other members of Muslim Brotherhood (*Ikhwanal-Muslimun*). Another important writer was Abul A'la Maududi, the

---

[6] Abduh was one of the most prominent figures of Islamic reformism in Egypt. In Indonesia his ideas deeply influenced the Islamic reformist movement, Muhammadiyah.

founder and the leader of *Jama'at al-Islami* (Islamic Group) in Pakistan.[7] Those books emphasised at least three major points. First, they attempted to re-examine Islam, and they tried to correct the view of Islam previously held by Muslims. In addition, they proposed Islam as a solution for all problems faced by Muslims. This led to their rejection of other ideologies, including socialism, nationalism and other 'isms'. Compared with other Muslim groups, they were more concerned with *aqidah* (basic faith), basic meanings of Islam, and the social and political aspects of Islam. These three aspects, in terms of approach, were quite radical and different from mainstream Islam. This was a crucial factor in the development of the movement.

Aqidah (basic faith), for young activists, is the most important aspect of Islam because it is the foundation of all activities and determines people's lives. An informant said that like a foundation of a house, it determines the strength of the building. Although the building is made from very good material, it would be ruined if its foundation was fragile. *Aqidah*, therefore, is conceived as comprehensive and basic thought about the universe, mankind and life, and it becomes a base of all activities. At this point Islam is identified as an ideology which opposes the established ideologies of Capitalism and Socialism.[8]

Based on my interviews with many Muslim activists, I found similar views that Islam is not only a belief and ritual system, but also includes law (*Syari'ah*), politics and way of life (*nizham*). Islam, according to this view, is a complete code of life which rules all aspects of life, including individual, social, economical, political and cultural life. This implies that Islam is conceived as not only a setof beliefs and a socio-political code but also a cultural code.

This new cultural view of Islam emerged as a result of dissatissfaction not only with the established social and political order, which oppressed Islamic social ideas and political aspirations, but also against the cultural order. From their historical perceptions, Muslim activists believed that Islam and Muslims often became victims of corrupt leaders and a bad system. They asserted that Western cultural infiltration through mass media, both printing and electronic, had "intoxicated" the Muslim *ummat*, especially young Muslim generations. The general trend among youngsters who often regarded everything which came

---

[7] Some titles of these books are *This Religion of Islam, Al-Islam, Towards Understanding Islam, The Future for Islam, Islam the Misunderstood Religion, Islam and Universal Peace, Iman dan 20 Perkara yang Membatalkan Syahadatain* (Faith and 20 Matters which Nullify the Profession of Faith), and *Jundullah Jihad Fi Sabilillah* (The Soldier of God's War in the way of God).

[8] Other religions such as Christianity, Judaism and Budhism, in the view of Muslims activists, do not cover all aspects of human life. Christians, for example, believe that Christianity the religio taught by Jesus Christ is universal. However, in the Muslim activists' view, it does not havecomplete rules by which all dimensions of life of the Christians must be ruled by the Christian teachings. In Christianity there is a division of spiritual and temporal (wordly) life. It was knownthat in Christianity there is a doctrine "Render unto Caesar the things which are Caesar's and to God the things which are God's." Likewise, Buddhism also accepts the dichotomy of life, spiritual and worldly life (Rais 1985:27–48).

from the West (*Barat*, America and Europe) as good, for Muslim activists was a clear evidence of "Westoxication."[9] This 'westoxication,' they believed, created a permissive and valueless society resulting in moral decadence. Indonesia, as Imaduddin puts it, was a place to be cleansed because it was full of injustice and un-Islamic practices (Naipaul 1981:350:2).

Another implication of the idea that Islam is a complete code of life is that Islam does notneed any other ideas from other sources. It does not need assistance from other ideologies. Islam is self sufficient. This view leads to a total rejection of any other value systems, such as socialism, liberalism, communism, secularism and other 'isms'. An informant said that valuesystems or ideologies other than Islam are regarded as a source of chaos and conflict within Muslim society. The world, including Muslim countries, was dominated by those powers. Behind all of this, he further said, was the Zionist[10]power, which was always hostile to Islam.

The idea that Islam is a complete code of life also implies rejection of the division between the religious and non religious. Such division was often believed as a

[9] 'Westoxification,' 'Westoxication,' 'Westomania,' 'Occidentosis,' 'Westitis,' 'Euromania,' and 'Weststruckness' are terms translated from a book written by a modern Iranian novelist and social critic Jalal al-e Ahmad *Gharbzadegi*. According to Madjid Tehranian (1993), Westoxication is the right translation because it "connotes a richer meaning in English in that the individual so addicted, just like any intoxicated individual, enjoys the conditions of his own addiction." This book became a major source of ideological inspiration for the revolution, and because of this, the book was banned after its first publication in 1963. After the revolution it was distributed widely throughout the country, and the title of the book *Gharbzadegi* became a phrase for the malaise of modern Iranian society. The core idea of this book is that the West has never been a panacea, but rather is a terrible disease which has poisoned Iranian society. In his *Gharbzadegi* (English translation by John Green and Ahmad Alizadeh *Westruckness*, Lexington: Mazda 1982), Jalal al-E Ahmad criticised the Western developmentalist policies of the Shah's regime. He argues that Western neocolonialism often penetrated the minds and souls of the nations of the Third World through a pathology called 'Westoxication,' a total irrational fascination with everything Western at the expense of the indigenous cultural heritage. Furthermore, he discovered Western intentions to destroy Islamic unity and the involvement of the Shahin this endeavour. At the same time he also argued that 'Eastoxication' is pathological obsession among intellectuals with Marxist and communist ideologies. While they were negating religion as 'the opium of the masses,' intentionally or not these intellectuals disconnected themselves from the masses and on the contrary they served the interests of the colonial powers of the Soviet Union. Based on these negative valuations of West and East, came the slogan, which later became the slogan of the Islamic Republic of Iran, 'Neither East nor West, Islam is best' (*La sharqiyya wa la gharbiyya illa al-Islam*) (Tehranian 1993:341–73, and Rajaee 1993:103–25). This term 'Westoxication" has been used as a powerful rhetoric of various Islamic movements throughout the Muslim world. The term Westoxication itself emerged and developed for the first time in Iran, but the idea that Muslims had been intoxicated by Western values and culture has been a common theme among those Islamic movements.

[10] Zionism, according to Ismail R. al-Faruqi (1983), a professor of Islamic studies in Temple University, America, refers to "a movement launched by Theodore Herzl following his disillusionment by the Dreyfus Affair. It was designed to transform Palestine and its adjacent territoriesinto a Jewish state, 'as Jewish as England is English.' Its pursuit of this objective is thoroughly Machiavellian. Its single-minded purpose is given absolute priority over all considerations, including the moral" (p.261–267). This term 'Zionist,' like 'Westoxication,' was a common rhetoric label among young Muslim activists for those who were believed as hostile to Islam.

symptom of secularism[11] an ideology that only thinks about and binds itself to this present life and rejects the existence of the hereafter. "Secular people seem to be good, their pragmatic actions make them forget future (hereafter) matters. At the extreme level, they will do anything to reach their goals" (Imaduddin 1980:36). Islam, according to Imaduddin (an important figure of the youth Islamic resurgence in Bandung) is a way of life which rules all of human activities, and therefore none of our lives should be profane or non-religious. He explains that Islam even prescribes what to do on going to the toilet. A Muslim for example, is supposed to say a prayer (*do'a*) and enter the toilet with the left foot. He further says, "keep our body healthy so that we can carry out God's order and obey God much better, this is *ibadah* (worship) (*Ibid*, p.47). By this he rejects the translation of the word *al-Din* in *al-Din al-Islam* as 'religion' (*agama*) because *al-din*, for Imaduddin, means a complete way of life whereas 'religion' is merely a set of beliefs and rituals (cf. Lyon 1979:37).

Finally, the notion of Islam as a complete code of life led to the idea of an Islamic state. It was commonly believed that the totality of Islam can only be comprehensively applied in a system or state which is also completely Islamic. Among the Islamic youth resurgence movement, there are at least two different groups. There are some groups who believe that the present regime is nottotally un-Islamic, but changes to be more Islamic are necessary. Other groups believe that the present regime is completely un-Islamic, and should be changed by revolution to Islam. Because Islam, as Mursalin Dahlan explains, cannot be applied partially. In his view, there are only two choices accepting Islam completely or rejecting it completely. He further says "Believing or practising some parts of Islam and rejecting the others is *kafir* (infidel). Islam should be accepted completely (*kaaffah*) or rejected completely." This was the view of Islamic underground movements, such as the Young DI (Darul Islam) and LP3K (Pesantren Kilat Movement) movement, whereas the former view was held by the formal Islamic movements, such as those at public mosques and campus preaching institutions.

Their notion of a more Islamic and a completely Islamic state refers to the ideal period of Islam in the era of the Prophet and his companions. It was believed, by most Muslim activists, that the Prophet established a state which was built on the basis of God's revelations. In this state, Muslims rule themselves with Islamic law (*shariat*) which covered all aspects of life. This ideal conception of an Islamic state, among the Islamic youth resurgence movement created two

[11] Secularisation processes refer to "the separation of the state from the church leading in its advanced stage to the separation of politics from religion, ...[ie.] the disestablishmentof religion in the domain of public policy and its relegation to the realm of private preference and judgement. ...[As a result of] the demonstrated and incontrovertible success of rationalism in various areas of life, religion would eventually lose its salience even for the individual.... Thus secularism refers to both eradication of religion as an institution in human society and erosion of man's faith in the divine and the trascendental (Haq 1986:332–3).

aims: to establish an Islamic state, and to apply Islamic law. These aims, as in other Islamic resurgence movements in the world have been the two main characteristics of contemporary Islamic movements, namely "legalist" (the comprehensive application of Islamic law, *shariat*) and "autonomist," or "separatist" (the establishment of an Islamic state) (cf. Pipes 1980:17–39). In Pakistan, for example, the Islamic movement demanded the application of Islamic law, whereas in Sudan, in the Southern Philippines, and in Kashmir, Islamic movements demanded an Islamic state and full autonomy.

To establish an Islamic state and a more Islamic identity, Muslim activists believed they had to prepare the Muslim *ummat* so they could accept Islam as their law. Furthermore, this preparation process could only be achieved through *jihad* [12] (endeavour, holy war) and *dakwah* [13] (proselytisation). According to an informant, the spirit of *jihad* had disappeared from the hearts of Muslims. It was not surprising then when *jihad* became an important subject among young Muslim activists.

Among some groups of Muslims I interviewed, there was an awareness that it was impossible toreach the above aims without collective efforts. They believed that there should be a cohesive group (*jama'ah*), who was expected to be the pioneer of the *dakwah* (Islamic preaching) movements. This belief, they claimed, is based on the examples of the Prophet in the early phases of development of Islam. The Prophet Muhammad, according to an informant, established a small group secretly in a companion's house. Arqam's house became a secret centre of the early Islamic movement, from which members of the groups spread to preach Islam secretly. This period was named by some groups as the Mecca period, or a period of forming cadres. Based on this view, some Muslim groups believe that they shouldestablish a *jama'ah* which spreads Islam secretly. These groups later developed as underground movements. Interpretation of the history of early Islam of the Prophet varied among the Muslim groups, and in the later developments, this became a source of disagreement among the Islamic youth resurgence movements.

From the above description there are three important issues. First, the idea that Islam as a complete code of life which provides answers for all questions of modern life is quite different from what was previously conceived. Previously, the Islamic movement was a purification movement which attempted to purify Islamic teachings and to refute local un-Islamic traditions. In the following phase, Islamic movements had a more political character. Finally, contemporary Islamic

---

[12] The word *jihad* is an Arabic word meaning fight, battle and holy war against the infidels. The root of this word is *jahada* which means to endeavour and to strive, and because of this the word *jihad* often translated into Indonesian as "endeavour" (*berusaha dengan sungguh-sungguh*)

[13] The term *dakwah* comes from the Arabic word *da'wa* which is from the root *da'a*, meaning to call or invite, ie. to call mankind to Islam. Dakwah also means missionary activities, ie. Islamic evangelism which promotes Islamic teachings among Muslims.

youth resurgence movements have been less concerned with Islamic purification and Islamic politics, and more concerned with the cultural aspects of Islam. Despite these differences, contemporary Islamic movements and previous Islamic movements have something in common ie. all of them try to make Islam present and felt in society and to give Islam substance and a role in society (Bahasoan 1985:131–60). At this point, the current Islamic movements seem to be a continuation of previous Islamic movements.

Second, through the translation of many books which later became a reference for various groups of Islamic movement, ideas developed by various Islamic youth resurgence movements in Bandung, and generally in Indonesia, were highly influenced by other Islamic movements throughout the world, especially in the Middle East. Among others, the thought of the *Ikhwan al-Muslimin* in Egypt, and *Jamaat-i-Islami* in Pakistan were the most influential sources for the Islamic youth resurgence movement in Bandung in its early development. This international influence was not only in terms of ideas but also in terms of motivation.

2.5 International Influences

Islamic reformist movements in Indonesia have always had connections with other Islamic movements in other parts of the world. The emergence of reformist movements, such as Muhammadiyah and PERSIS, was deeply influenced by the Islamic movements in the Middle East, such as Wahabism in Saudi Arabia, and the Islamic reform movement of Muhammad Abduh (1849–1905) and Jamaluddin al-Afghani (1839–1897) in Egypt. Like previous Islamic movements in Indonesia, contemporary Islamic youth resurgence movements in Indonesia are also influenced by international Islamicmovements.

Different from their predecessors, current Islamic movements developed in an era of globalisation, in which mass communication technology has been revolutionised. Recent advances of technology have led to a situation where citizens of the planet earth are linked inextricably by satellites, receiver dishes, transmitters and cable television networks and relays. At this stage, all humans are in one community, a global community (Shupe 1990:17–26) or in McLuhan and Fiore's (1968) term a "global Village." This situation, in relation to the Islamic movement, creates a closer connection among various Islamic movements.

Previously, the influence of the international Islamic movement reached Indonesia after a period of time. Usually, the founders of the Indonesian movements met reformist ideas in the Middle East when they studied Islam or when they did pilgrimage (*hajj*) in Mecca. When they returned to Indonesia they preached their reformists ideas and later established a movement. For this reason, there was a time lapse which differentiated the Islamic movement in other parts of the world and the Islamic movements in Indonesia. The agents of these movement were individuals. In later developments, this agency of change was also through books and other printed media. Finally, the agency of the contemporary Islamic movement is not only through individuals and printed media but also through various electronic mass communication media, such as television networks and direct broadcasting systems. This advance of telecommunication technology has revolutionised the spread of ideas and information. What is on television in America can also be seen at the same time in a small village in Bandung, Indonesia. Through television, what happens in other parts of Islamic world can immediately be seen and heard by Muslims in Indonesia.

This fast current of information is very important in understanding the emergence and early development of the Islamic youth resurgence movement in Indonesia, especially in Bandung. One of the most important international events which greatly influenced the early development of the movement was the Islamic revolution in Iran in1979. This event for Muslim activists had three impacts. First, it gave Muslim activists the idea of an Islamic revolutionary movement and that Islam could become a radical ideology which could challenge established ideologies. Second, Islamic revolution in Iran psychologically motivated Muslim activists and convinced them that they could also succeed like the Islamic movement led by Khomeini in Iran. Third, the Islamic revolution in Iran also influenced the way Muslim females wore clothes or at least reinforced the teaching of the veil (*kerudung, jilbab*) This was because female Muslims who supported the revolution in Iran wore the veil and black clothes.

In the late 1970s and early 1980s, these influences could be seen clearly. There was a kind of admiration toward Khomeini as the leader of the revolution. The portrait of Khomeini was hung in young Muslim activists' rooms and in offices of student and youth Muslim organisations. Another influence could be identified clearly in the way Muslim female activists wore clothes. In the late1970 s there were very few female Muslims who wore the veil, however in the early 1980s-just one or two years after the Islamic revolution in Iran- those who wore the veil increased rapidly. Furthermore, the distinct Iranian influence was that Muslim female activists wore black veil and clothes similar to those female activists in Iran.

The influence of the revolution in Iran was reinforced by the translation of books written by important revolutionary figures. The works of some Shi'ite scholars, such as Ali Shariati and Imam Khomeini were published and read by Sunni Muslim people in Indonesia. Along with other books written by Sunni scholars, such as Sayyid Qutb, Hasan al-Banna and Mawlana Maududi, these books shaped a new Muslim view on Islam.

These impacts of the Islamic revolution in Iran on the early development of Islamic youth resurgence movement are clear despite the fact that the revolution in Iran was a revolution of the Shi'ite (*Si'ah*) Muslims. It is a quite interesting fact that regardless of differences,[14] Indonesian Sunni Muslims accepted revolutionary ideas from the Shi' ite Muslims in Iran. An informant says, "we do not agree with some of the faith and teachings of the Shi' ite, but we have learnt from the revolutionary ideas of the Shi'ite." At this stage, as Khurshid Ahmad (1983) says, the contemporary Islamic movement reached a very important phase in Muslim history marked by its non- sectarian characteristic (p.223).

2.6 The Founder: An Individual Background

It is not easy for me to decide which Islamic institutions played the most important role in the emergence of the Islamic revivalism among the young people in Indonesia, especially in Bandung. As I focused my study on the Islamic revivalism among young people, including students from the mid-1970s to early 1990s, I studied the case among the university campuses. During this period Islamic activities in almost all university campuses began to take shape. Public and campus mosques were crowded by young people, most of them students. They came to pray (*sholat*), attend public sermons (*pengajian*) and take part other activities. This was followed by the 'veil (*kerudung* or *jilbab*) movement'. Female university students and later senior high school students started to wear head cover.

In Bandung, Salman Mosque at the ITB (Bandung Institute of Technology)[15] was the first Islamic institution in which Islamic activities for young people were held in a proper organisation. That Salman Mosque with its Karisma organisation was the most influential Islamic institution in the Islamic youth resurgence movement in Bandung and in Indonesia, was reported by V.S. Naipaul who visited Bandung in the late 1970s. Naipaul observed that Bandung is "one of centres of the Islamic revival in Indonesia" (1981:338). Thousands of young people from Jakarta, Bogor and other cities in Indonesia came to attend a short Islamic course, which he called 'mental training', at Salman Mosque at The Bandung Institute of Technology (ITB, Institut Teknologi Bandung). The course was given by Imaduddin, an electrical engineer, a lecturer at the institute, who had also graduated from the ITB. Imaduddin is one of the most important figures involved in the establishment of the Salman Mosque, and in general in the emergence of Islamic youth resurgent movement in Bandung.

His full name was Muhammad Imaduddin Abdulrahim. Among young people, he was called Bang Imad.[16] He was born in 1931 to a devout Muslim family in

[14] Sunni or *Ahl al-Sunna* (People of the Sunna) refers to those Muslims who uphold customs based on the practice and authority of the Prophet and his companions, as distinct from *Shi'a* ('the party' of Ali) which comprising those Muslim who uphold the rights of 'Ali and his descendants to leadership of the Ummah.
[15] ITB is one of the most, prestigious tertiary institution in Indonesia, having produced many national leaders, including Soekarno, the first president.
[16] Bang is an intimate name, meaning big brother. Usually used in Jakarta and some other regions in Sumatra.

Medan, North Sumatra. His mother was from a noble family of the Riau Sultanate. Because of his mother's position, he could enter the Dutch School, HIS (Hollandsch Inlandische School) which only recruited children from noble and aristocrat families (*Ulumul Qur'an* 2:5:94). His father was a religious teacher, who graduated from Al-Azhar Islamic University, Cairo, Egypt. He was one of the teachers of a famous religious school (*madrasah*) run by the sultanate in the Dutch time. At this school, he was also one of the principals (Naipaul 1981:345). In the political sphere, Imaduddin's father was one of the leaders of Masyumi, representing his region, North Sumatra. Moreover, in the Council of the Muslim Clergy he had the highest position, as a *qadi* (Muslim judge) (Naipaul 1981:347 and *Ulumul Qur'an*, 2:5:94).

During the revolution against the Dutch, Imaduddin was involved in the Muslim Army Hizbullah.[17] At the age of fifteen, in 1946, he was trained as a guerilla fighter, and he received a star and a stripe as a first sergeant. In 1953, he finished his high school with the highest mark. While he was a student in Medan, he was one of the leaders of thestudents in his school. After finishing high school he continued his study in ITB. His ideal of becoming an electrical engineer was deeply influenced by Dr. Hatta's speech on his visit to the largest waterfall close to Medan. In his speech Hatta, who was then the vice president, stressed the importance of electricity (Naipaul 1981:346).

In 1953 he found Bandung and especially ITB a secular place. He found it difficult to find any mosque around the institute. The closest mosque was about three kilometres away. Before 1957, when Sukarno threw the Dutch out, almost all lecturers and professors in the institute were Dutch, and most of the lectures were presented in English. On his first Friday, Imaduddin was shocked by the fact that some classes took place during prayer time. Since he was brought up in a strict Muslim family, absence from Friday prayer in the mosque was quite a mental shock for Imaduddin. He asked permission to go to the mosque. The lecturer allowed him and his three friends to go. He went tothe mosque but he missed the lecture. This happened every Friday. He felt that the campus was dry ofreligious activities.[18] He became inspired by the idea of having a mosque close to the campus (Naipaul 1981:347)

[17] It means the party of Allah, a military unit for the Muslim youth, established by the Japanese at the end of 1944. Ulamas and Muslim leaders also established Sabilillah (the way of Allah) which acted as the main body and protector for Hizbullah. From the Japanese point of view, it was a strategy to defeat the alliesu, and a realisation of Nippon's Islamic Grass roots Policy (Benda 1958:134). In addition, the Japanese realised that the ulamas and the Islamic leaders were not only formal leaders but also very influential figures in the Muslim community (Ma' arif 1985:99).

[18] Interview with Imaduddin. A similar feeling was also experienced by Mursalin Dahlan. According to Mursalin Dahlan, the campus environment with all its aspects made him thirsty for religious situations, which he was used to. This was because at that period, between 1950s and 1960s, one's religion was always identified as a political alliance. As a result of this, people, especially Muslims who performed prayer five times a day, were unwilling to show their ritual performances. Furthermore, in the ITB at

When he entered the ITB he became involved in HMI (Islamic Student Association). In1954 he was appointed as a head of education and preaching (*dakwah*) of the HMI Bandung region. This position forced him to organise various training activities for members of the organisation. His experience in managing training activities later inspired him to hold similar activities in Salman Mosque.

One year after he finished his study in 1961, he became a lecturer in the Institute. Later, beside teaching his discipline, ie. electrical engineering, he also taught the Religion of Islam.[19] In 1963 he was involved in the committee for the development of the Salman mosque, in which he served as deputy chairman. He also held Islamic discussions and *pengajian* (religous lecture). Gradually, his preachings attracted audiences who not only came from among the ITB students but also young people and students from surrounding areas. In the same year, ITB sent him to the United States to get his masters' degree. He studied there for three years at Iowa State University.

After finishing his study in 1965, he was asked to return to Indonesia to teach again at the ITB as some of the lecturers had been involved in 30 th September Communist movement (G30 S PKI) and were dismissed. On his return to Indonesia, HMI held a National Congress in Solo. Knowing that Imaduddin had returned, the congress nominated him as the head of Preaching Institution of Islamic Students (LDMI,*Lembaga Dakwah Mahasiswa Islam*). Through this position he met Nurcholish Madjid (now a celebrated Indonesian Muslim intellectual), Abdul Latief (now the Minister of Employment) and Mar'ie Muhammad (now the Finance Minister). From that timehe regularly held training activities for university students, which he called LKD (*Latihan Kader Dakwah*, Preaching Cadre Training) and later changed into LMD (*Latihan Manajemen Dakwah*, Preaching Management Training).

In 1970, the Malaysian Minister of Education came to ITB Bandung and with his group joined Friday prayer. Imaduddin was, at that time, the *imam* and the *khatib*. Interested in Imaduddin' s methods of Islamic education, the minister asked him to come to Malaysia to encourage Islamic resurgence, as Imaduddin had done in Indonesia.[20] He happily agreed to the request, and in 1971 he went to Malaysia as a lecturer from the ITB, under the auspices of the Indonesian Ministry of Education (Imaduddin 1990:xvi–vii).

---

that time only very few of students and academic staffs came from *santri* (more a committed Muslim) background.
[19] According to Mursalin Dahlan, religion subjects, especially Islam, had never been taught in the Institute until1962. Nowadays, all religions are taught in all universities, and all students are free to choose any religions they want to studythe establishment of University of Technology Malaysia (UTM).
[20] According to Naipaul, when Imaduddin was at Cornell University he met a Malaysian, through whom in 1971 he went to Malaysia to help

The first thing he did in Malaysia was to propose that Islamic subjects be included in the university curriculum, as had been done in Indonesia in 1962. While he was teaching at the University of Technology Malaysia (UTM) in Kuala Lumpur, he also conducted religious talks for selected groups of Malay students, whom he felt had leadership qualities, at different campuses in Kuala Lumpur. Students regarded him as a powerful and convincing orator who could awaken awareness in his audiences of their wrongdoing. According to Shukran Jamel Zaini, a dakwah leader, "[Imaduddin] made us realise the gravity of our wrongdoing and that we could not carry out a dichotomous life when we believe that Islam is a complete way of life" (Anwar 1987:20).

In the middle of 1972, because of student enthusiasm for his teaching, he proposed a special Islamic course, organised during the semester holidays. The course lasted about four days and five nights, and was held in a *surau*.[21] The participants were limited to 40 students, and they had to pass an interview. Through this interview Imaduddin tried to select students who were not only clever but also had leadership talent. It was expected that after the course they would become the pioneers of the dakwah movement on university campuses. The course ended with *tahajud* (anoptional midnight prayer) and *bai'ah* (oath)[22] together before dawn (*subuh*). Imaduddin named this course LKD (*Latihan Kader Dakwah*, Preacher Cadre Training (Imaduddin 1990:xix–xx).

At UTM, he developed a core group of about 100 followers, many of whom later went to Britainto study and continued their dakwah activities. When they came back to Malaysia, with more committed zeal for Islam, they taught at various universities and other institutions in Malaysia (Anwar 1987:21). Their dakwah movement became much bigger and stronger, especially when they had higher positions in the places where they worked. One of the students trained by Imaduddin was Anwar Ibrahim, who now is a leader of UMNO (United Malays National Organisation) party and Deputy Prime Minister.

The link with an Indonesian Muslim activist was as an important impetus to Islamic resurgence in Malaysia. This link in fact was started when HMI (Himpunan Mahasiswa Islam Indonesia, Muslim Students' Association) helped ABIM (*Angkatan Belia Islam Malaysia*, Muslim Youth Movement of Malaysia) and PKPIM (*Persatuan Kebangsaan Pelajar-Pelajar Islam Malaysia*, National Association of Muslim Students Malaysia) to organise several Islamic training trips to Jakarta and Bandung. The HMI leaders helped ABIMto formulate ideas

---

[21] Surau is a prayer house, communal building suitable for any prayers except Friday prayer.

[22] The meaning of *Bai'ah* here is very different from the *bai'ah* in the period of the Prophet or *bai'ah* in the Sufi Orders. In the above case, the participants only say a prayer or even only read a poem, which is led by an instructor. The word 'bai'ah'in fact has very broad meanings. It derives from *ba'a* which mean to sell. *Baya'a*, to make the *bay'a*, in Arabic grammar called musyarakah, mutual, in which two parties are bond together by rights and obligations. Therefore, the above case, according to Jalaluddin Rakhmat, is not bai'ah.

and arguments against the Nationalist and Socialist forces in their universities and in the government (Anwar 1987:18–19).

Imaduddin stayed in Malaysia until he was 'returned' (*dikembalikan*) to Indonesia in September 1973. In his view, the Malaysian authorities expelled him because of his critical attitude. When he first came to Malaysia, he was actually shocked by the act of a mufti (religious high judge) who kissed the hand of the Sultan. Finally, in the middle of July 1973 Imaduddin was invited to be a key note speaker at a big public sermon (*tabligh akbar*). In this sermon he criticised the hypocritical attitude of some leaders who were known as drunkards but regarded students who used drugs as criminal (Imaduddin 1990:xxiii).

His visit to Malaysia increased his interest in the international Muslim movement. He then visited Libya, England and Pakistan. Because of his wide connections and his position in the Islamic Student Association (HMI) as the head of the Islamic Student Preaching Institution (*Lembaga Dakwah Mahasiswa Islam, LDMI*) he was nominated to be a secretary of the International Islamic Federation of Student Organisations (IIFSO) (Naipaul 1981:349 and Aziz 1989:217). In the name of this organisation, he held or sponsored LMD (*Latihan Manajemen Dakwah*) type of training in many Islamic organisations in Australia, Korea, Hongkong and Europe (*Ulumul Qur'an* 2:5:94). This organisation linked him more closely to the ideas of the Muslim Brotherhood (*Ikhwanul Muslimin*) movement, which was established by Hasan Al-Banna in Egypt. He also gained contact with other Islamic movements such as *Jami'at Islami* founded by Abul A'la Maududi in Pakistan. It is not surprising that his view of Islam was deeply influenced by these movements.

In 1974, a year after he returned from Malaysia, he held LMD (*Latihan Manajement Dakwah*) training in Salman Mosque of ITB, but with a small change, ie. from *Latihan Managemen Dakwah* into *Latihan Mujahid Dakwah* (Dakwah Warrior Training).[23] At this time he was no longer the head of Islamic Student Preaching Institution (LDMI) of the HMI, because after the 10th HMI congress in Palembang in 1971, the LDMI was removed from the HMI structure (HMI 1972), and Imaduddin no longer held a central position in the institution (Aziz 1989:218).

Latihan Mujahid Dakwah training activity was the embryo of the development of Islamic intensification groups in Salman Mosque of ITB and in the Bandung area which have continued until now. The LMD was originally aimed to create a breakthrough in the development of Islam, especially in the ITB. It formed cadres of Islamic preachers who became pioneers of the development of Islam.

---

[23] According to Imaduddin, his idea to hold such activities was inspired by the book *Mujahid Dakwah* (Dakwah Warrior) written by Isa Anshary, an important Masyumi and PERSIS figurein Bandung. Imaduddin further explains, his experience while he was in America, especially when he attended missionary training, was also infuential (*Ulumul Qur'an* 2:5:94).

To achieve this, at least three aspects were stressed: basic knowledge of Islam, implantation of the spirit of struggle, and commitment to the group. The first aspect was related to the basic information (and some misconceptions) about Islam and its teachings. Problems faced by Muslim *Ummat* were introduced and discussed to develop participants' awareness and responsibility. Moreover, it encouraged participants to struggle for Islam. The training, which lasted one or two weeks continuously, was ended with a *bai'at*, an oath as an inauguration. With the *bai'at*, the collective determination of theparticipants to spread the mission was strengthened.

Since LMD was considered as training to form preacher cadres, all participants had to pass through a selection in the form of an interview. The selection was based on participants' Islamic knowledge, personality, motivation, aims and their attitude towards the program. Moreover, theintellectual potential of the participants, specifically shown by the cumulative marks of the students (*Indeks Prestasi, IP*), was considered. For the ITB students, for example, the minimal IP was 2.75. Therefore the aim of the training, i. e. to form cadres withthe qualities of faith and morals, combined with scientific and intellectual abilities was clear in the first stage of training (Aziz 1989:268–9).

In 1979 the name of the training program was changed to Intensive Islamic Study (SII). On the one hand, this can be seen as a broadening of the program, in terms of target and time. On the other hand, this was the only way to keep the training going in the face of external pressure. According to Imaduddin, there were hostile feelings, especially from military authorities, with regardto the word '*mujahid*,' in *Latihan Mujahid Dakwah*.[24] This is because the word Interview with Imaduddin, 8 March 1994. '*mujahid*,' which means warrior, fighter and one who fights in a holy war, has a rebellious connotation (like *Komando Jihad* rebellion) and often implies the idea of an Islamic state (Darul Islam, DI). In 1978 he was accused of being anti- Pancasila, anti- Christian and not being nationalist, and because of these accusations he was detained for14 months.[25] Afterthis detention he was not allowed to teach at the ITB, and in 1980 he went to America to continue his study for a PhD degree. In 1986 he returned to Indonesia, but he could not go back to the ITB because he had been fired by his dean (*Ulumul Qur'an* 2:5:94).

In Imaduddin' s view for the umpteenth time he became a victim of corrupt leaders and a bad system. Indonesia for Imaduddin was a place to be cleansed, and it was full of injustice and therefore un-Islamic. The ideal for him was an Islamic state, as it was practiced in the era of the Prophet and his four Caliphates.

---

[24] Interview with Imaduddin, 8 March 1994.

[25] According to Imaduddin, he was arrested only because of the BAIS (Badan Intelejen dan Strategis, Intellegence and Strategic Bureau) action which controlled by Benni Murdani and his groups. For Imaduddin, BAIS was not *Badan Intelejen dan Strategis* but '*Badan Anti Islam*' (Anti-Islam Bureau).'

However, for Imaduddin, the Indonesian constitution had some Islamic values in it. 'What we need now is the people behind the structure. They must be true Muslims'. He believed that what was needed now was a true Muslim leader, 'who lived according to the Quran, ... who could stand in for the Prophet, ... who knew the Prophet' s deeds so well that he would order affairs as the Prophet himself might have ordered them' (Naipaul 1981:350–2). For this reason, Imaduddin was concerned with Islamic education for youngsters.

During his second time in America, he often met and discussed issues with Muslim intellectuals, such as Nurcholis Madjid, Amin Rais and Syafi'i Ma'arif, who also studied in America. From these discussions emerged an idea to unite Muslim intellectuals in Indonesia. On his return he tried to promote his idea through various activities but always failed. However, in1990 his idea became a reality when a symposium of Muslim intellectuals was held in the Brawijaya University Malang, from which Indonesian Muslim Intellectuals Association (*ICMI, Ikatan Cendekiawan Muslim se-Indonesia*) was born.

From Imaduddin's individual background emerge four important issues. First, Imaduddinisan example of those who came from strong Islamic circles in rural areas and then moved to a city, in which modernisation and Western (Dutch) institutions clearly existed. Living in the Westernised and secularised milieu of the ITB (at the time when most of its lecturers were European) he missedthe 'religious' environment he was used to. Second, Imaduddin's critical view of the social and political situation led him to pseudo-political opposition to a suppressiveand strict political system. Through various small group forums and Islamic training among the university students, Imaduddin spread his political perceptions and at the same time his theological and Islamic ideas, which often supported one another. These discussion groups and training institutions later provided a shelter for various students movements banned in 1979. Furthermore, these institutions became a center of Muslim student activists who were not satisfied with established Islamic student organisations. Such a tendency emerged, I believe, because student movements and Islamic youth movements have something in common, namely their social and political criticism of the existing regime. Third, it is clear that Imaduddin's Islamic and political ideas were influenced by various Islamic movements throughout the world such as *Ikhwanal-Muslimin* (Muslim Brethren) in Egypt and *Jamaat-i-Islami* (Islamic society) in Pakistan. His meeting in international Islamic forums led him to know more about other Islamic movements and other political and Islamic ideas. Furthermore, Imaduddin was deeply involved in the early emergence of the Islamic youth resurgence movement in Malaysia, when he helped the foundation of ABIM (Muslim Youth Movement of Malaysia). Finally, without neglecting the roles of other figures or institutions, Imaduddin was a charismatic figure, a convincing radical and a brave person (cf. Anwar 1987:19–27) who played a significant role in the early emergence of Islamic youth resurgence movement in Bandung, and perhaps in Indonesia.

In conclusion, this analysis has focused on the factors contributing to religious resurgenceespecially among young people. First, there is social dissatisfaction and frustration -notonly in terms of social, economic and political subordination but also in terms of spiritual or religious deprivation- experienced by some part of society. This dissatisfaction is an accumulation of a long period of unfulfilled expectation. Second, this social dissatisfaction is initially experienced only by a few individual members of society, by whom the idea of dissatisfaction is spread to the wider part of the society. Very few of these individual members are charismatic[26] figures who are able to convince and spread the idea to other people. Third, the nature of youth which is radical, critical and rebellious toward the *status quo* became a significant factor for the early emergence of the movement. Finally, there are some events or issues which triggered the initial emergence of the movement. These events do not occur only at local or national level but also at the international level.

[26] Borrowing Weber's definition of charisma, it refers to "a certain quality of an individual personality by virtue of which [one] is set apart from ordinary men and treated as endowed with supernatural, superhuman, or at least specifically exceptional powers or qualities. These are such as are not accessible to the ordinary person, but are regarded as of divine origin or as exemplary, and on the basis of them the individual concerned is treated as a leader" (1947:358–9). This definition does not mean that Imaduddin or other founders had superhuman quality or had miraculous or magical ability. Instead, by charisma here I refer to a personality characteristicwhich is regarded as extraordinary. Those who posses it are thought and regarded by their followers to have extraordinary qualities which cannot be acquired by ordinary persons (Gerth 1969:258).

Chapter 3: The Development of the Movement

3.1 Introduction

"Religion is like a nail. The harder you hit it, the deeper it goes into the wood" (Emerson, 1981:159).

The second stage, the focus of this chapter, is the development of the Islamic resurgence movement among young people. The important feature of this period is the spread of Islamic resurgence ideas through communication and evangelism, either by persuasive individuals, or through various sorts of mass gatherings. To assist an understanding of this process, I attend to two aspects of the development: the organisations through which the movement developed, focusing on public mosques, campus Islamic preaching organisations, and Islamic movements; and the social phenomena which challenged or accelerated the development of the movement during the 1980s.

3.2 Three Channels: Campus Islamic Preaching Organisations, Public Mosques, and Underground Movements

In the early 1980s, as reported by *Panji Masyarakat*,[1] youngsters all over the country became much more familiar with mosques. This was a new phenomenon. Mosques were crowded by young people, especially during the month of Ramadan. They spent much of their time in mosques. They came to mosques not only to pray *tarawih* (an optional night prayer during Ramadan) and *subuh* (morning prayer) but also to attend religious sermons, scientific discussions (*diskusi ilmiah*), recitation of the Qur'an and to attend other activities held during the day. Such phenomena could be seen in large and small public mosques in most big cities of Indonesia. It was estimated that approximately 2,000 mosques conducted such activities. Young Muslims active in these mosques began to form mosque organisations for young people (*Ikatan Remaja Mesjid* and *Pemuda Mesjid*).

University and school mosques were different from public mosques. In terms of organisational structure, they were, directly or indirectly, attached to the universities or schools where they were located. Therefore the chiefs of the mosques could only be university staff or students, whereas in public mosques there was no such requirement. Moreover, on some campuses, religious activities were closely related to Islamic religion courses and were compulsory course components. The activities were specifically aimed at students and academic

---

[1] An Indonesian Islamic fortnightly magazine; 11 July 1982.

staff. Later, however, because university mosques offered various interesting activities, they were also attended by people from surrounding areas. Later these Islamic organisations within university campuses became known as *Lembaga Dakwah Kampus* (*LDK*, Campus Islamic Preaching Organisation)

Similar activities were also conducted by various Islamic groups known as *harakah* ('movement').[2] These *harakah* differed from others by conducting their activities secretly. These Islamic groups usually held their activities in their members' premises; for example, in homes, halls, and sports stadiums. Sometimes they used mosques, schools or other places, as organised by their members. Like other Islamic organisations, they held sermons (*pengajian*), small group discussions (*usrah*), short training courses and other activities. Those activities could only be attended by members who had completed certain training. Membership recruitment in these groups was achieved through personal approaches. They were also different from other Islamic organisations such as Muhammadiyah or HMI (*Himpunan Mahasiswa Islam*, Islamic Student Association) in a sense that they were not formally approved by the government, and they were not attached to other Islamic organisations.

In Bandung and generally in Indonesia, these three types of organisations -public mosques, campus preaching organisation and Islamic groups- played an important role as channels through which Islamic revivalism among young people developed. Representative of the first type are two of the most prominent public mosques in Bandung, ie. Istiqamah and Mujahidin mosque.[3] The second type, ie. the *Lembaga Dakwah Kampus* (*LDK*), is represented by three important campus mosques: Salman Mosque of ITB (Bandung Institute of Technology), Padjadjaran University (UNPAD) mosque, and Al-Furqan mosque of Bandung Teaching and Education Institute (IKIP, Institut Keguruan Ilmu Pendidikan). The third type is illustrated by *Lembaga Penelitian dan Pengembangan Pesantren Kilat* (*LP3K*, Research and Development Organisation of Islamic Education Short Course), which was also known as the Pesantren Kilat Movement, and Young *Darul Islam* (*DI Muda*).[4] There are other groups besides these. However, because of their exclusiveness, I was able to collect only general information about them. In the following section I describe the main types of organisations in turn, starting with university mosques, followed by public mosques and *harakah*.

---

[2] The word '*harakah*', came from Arabic *harakat al-Islamiyah*, meaning 'Islamic movement'.

[3] In Bandung, there are more than a hundred large public mosques (*Masjid Jami and Masjid Raya*), which are usually used for *Jum'at* prayer. However, only a few of them are used as centres for young Islamic activists. The functioning of these two mosques, I believe, provides an understanding of the role of public mosques in the development of the Islamic revivalist movement among young people. Moreover, due to practical limitations, I focused my oberservation only on these mosques.

[4] *Darul Islam* was an Indonesian Muslim rebellion movement, which aimed at establishing an Indonesian Islamic State (NII, Negara Islam Indonesia). *Dar al-Islam*, an Arabic word means Islamic house and family, and lands or territories under Islamic rule, as opposite of *Dar al-Harb*, the non-Muslim state, lands in which Islamic rules do not prevail.

3.2.1. a. Salman's Inspiration

The need for a mosque on the ITB campus emerged in 1950s, when academic staff and students who came from santri families began to feel that their campus did not provide for spiritual values, especially Islamic values. The need became much greater as the number of Muslim students with strong Islamic backgrounds increased every year. A committee was formed in 1960 to produce a mosque development plan. In 1960, Sukarno approved the plan, and he even named the proposed mosque 'Salman', the name of a Muslim technocrat in the Prophet's era. Three years later, building of the mosque commenced, and Salman Mosque was first used in 1972. In 1965 the management of the mosque was delegated to *Yayasan Pembina Mesjid Salman* (*YPM Salman*, Salman Mosque Development Foundation). Although this mosque is independently managed by the *YPM Salman*, almost all of the board are academic staff of the ITB.

The Salman Mosque is located on the north side of Bandung. It is quite different from other mosques in Bandung. The architecture of the mosque is unique, its roof being flat, without a dome. The walls on the three sides and the floor are made of wood, and this gives a shaded (*teduh*) impression. This impression is even stronger at night, the arrangement of lamps giving a soft lighting effect. There is a bright lamp only at the *mihrab* (the niche or chamber) located at the very front of the main praying room where the *imam* (leader) leads the prayers and *khatib* (preacher) gives speeches. The first floor is the main prayer room for women. Close to the mosque, there are toilets, a hall, the YPM Salman office, a student dormitory, a clinic, printing room, library, canteen, the Kharisma office, and the PAS office. Behind the mosque is Ganesa Park, which is always used for Karisma and PAS (*Pendidikan Anak-anak Salman*, Salman's Children's Education of) activities.

The popularity of Salman Mosque increased rapidly after 1974, when it was comanaged by "Sadali who is calm and Imaduddin who is furious" (Tempo, 13:5:1989). Among other things, what attracted young people to this mosque was the *Latihan Mujahid Dakwah* (*LMD*, Preacher Training), which was developed and engineered by Imaduddin. LMD was a type of Islamic training in which university students were trained for about seven days without contact with the outside world. During this training, students learned some basic teachings of Islam, such as the source of Islamic values, Qur'an and *Sunnah* (Tradition of the Prophet), and the Islamic faith (*Aqidah Islam*). Attracted to this kind of training, students from various universities in Bandung, Jakarta, Yogyakarta, Medan and other areas, came to the Salman Mosque. When they returned to their universities, they began to develop Islamic activities in their own universities. Not surprisingly, two or three years later (1976–77) Islamic activities mushroomed on university campuses throughout Java. In IPB (Bogor Institute of Agriculture), Islamic activities developed through the Islamic

Spirituality Bureau (Badan Kerohanian Islam, *BKI*). At the University of Indonesia (UI) Jakarta, the Arief Rahman Hakim Mosque was a centre of Islamic activities. In Gajah Mada University Yogyakarta, Islamic activities also developed through *Jama'ah Shalahuddin*.[5] Similar phenomena also spread widely in Surabaya and other cities outside Java.

 In 1979, LMD was expanded and renamed Islamic Intensive Study (Studi Islam Intensif, SII). This change, according to Imaduddin,[6] was because of government pressure, which in turn resulted in the stagnation of the LMD program. In addition, it was also an attempt to widen the program in terms of aims and time period (Aziz and Thokhah 1989:265). LMD was available only to university students. There was no opportunity for high school and junior high school students to attend such training. The birth of the SII program offered similar activities to school students. Other than training programs, Islamic activities for adolescents were held from 1976, although initially they were not well organised. Since September 1980, adolescent Islamic activities have been organised properly and given the name *Program Pembinaan Remaja* (Youth Education Program). Its activities included mentoring, *Bimbingan Test* (a preparation test before entering university), theatre, a singing group and other activities. A year later in 1981, the *Program Pembinaan Remaja* was renamed *Keluarga Remaja Islam Salman* (Salman Mosque Youth Association) or *Karisma*, the name which is still used.

One of the most important activities of *Karisma* is "mentoring", an obligatory activity for all participants. When it was first introduced, it was a unique form of Islamic education. Mentoring sessions involve groups of eight to fifteen students discussing a 'package' of Islamic subjects. The main mentoring activity is held every Sunday morning at six a.m, and lasts for two hours. It takes place inside a mosque and its surrounding areas. The session always begins with a recitation from the Qur'an and its Indonesian translation, followed by a short speech given by the mentor as an introduction to discussion. The members then discuss the planned topic. During the discussion, participants not only ask about religious matters, but also discuss personal and family problems. Most of the participants want Islamic solutions to the problems they face. During the mentoring program, a bond among the members themselves, and among members and the mentor, develops. They are encouraged to visit each other, and to get to know each other better. To achieve this, every month they hold an excursion, picnic, bush walking or some other relaxation activities.

The discussion is led by a mentor, who is also a resource person. To be a mentor, one should be a university student (not only set aside for ITB students), pass an interview and have attended mentor training. This opportunity attracted many

---

[5] *Jama'ah*, an Arabic meaning group or community. *Shalahuddin* (Saladin), a Muslim leader during the Crusades.
[6] Interview with Imaduddin 8 March 1994

students from various universities in the area of Bandung. From 1978 the number of participants and mentors increased gradually and reached a peak in 1985–86, when it was reported that there were 300 mentors (*Anggota Pembina*) from 25 universities in Bandung. Most of them (35%) were ITB students, followed by UNPAD (15%), IAIN (11%), IKIP (8%) and the remaining 25% from 20 other universities in Bandung. In the same year it was also reported that there were about 2,700 participants or ordinary members (*Anggota Biasa*). In terms of level of education, approximately 23% were university students, 57% Senior High School (SMA) students, and 20% Junior High School (SMP) students. Most university and school students involved in Karisma activities were usually involved or later became involved in Islamic activities on their campuses. In this way Islamic activities spread widely through university and school campuses throughout Bandung.

The mentoring program is divided into several groups based on age and level of education. "A" group, divided into four levels, is the first level of education for basic Islamic teachings. Included in this group are young people, fourteen years of age or junior high school students (*SMP, Sekolah Menengah Pertama*). In this group, the topics of discussion stress moral (*akhlaq*) education and basic rituals, such as prayer (*shalat*), religious alms (*zakat*), fasting (*puasa*) and pilgrimage (*haji*). Students learn about the meanings and functions of rituals, to recite prayer (*bacaan dan do'a-doa dalam shalat*) and the detailed rules for many rituals (*ibadah*). The *akhlaq* education portrays some ideal Islamic personages, for example the Prophet and his companions. Students, at this stage, learn proper Islamic behaviour toward God (Allah), people and other creatures. The aim of this stage is to lay a basic foundation for the development of Muslim personality.

Senior high school and university students complete a further six stages: I and II B, III and IV C, V D and VI E. Each stage lasts one semester, or twenty-seven weeks, and within three years a participant can complete all of them. During these stages students begin to learn Islamic teachings in more depth. The package of Islamic subjects consists of fourteen main themes, including 'Toward Understanding Islam', 'Qur'an as the Guide for Life', 'Islam and Sunnatullah (Law of Nature)', 'Sunnah' (example of the Prophet Muhammad) and 'Tjtihad',[7] 'Tawhid', 'Muslim Personality', 'Islamic Leadership', 'Islamic Society', 'Islamic Family', 'Long Life Education', 'Man' (*Manusia*), 'Dakwah' (Islamic Preaching), and 'Trace of The Prophet'. Material on these fourteen themes is published in the form of small guide books distributed to all mentoring participants a week beforehand.

---

[7] A term used in Islamic jurisprudence to designate the process of arriving at new judgments in a rule of law in a particular case by drawing conclusions from basic sources of Islam, ie. Qur'an and *hadits*, as opposed to acceptance of tradition

Besides the main activity of mentoring, participants are also involved in some "supporter" (*pendukung*) activities, usually held on days other than Sunday. One of the most important programs is the *Bimbingan Test*, a preparation course to enter top state universities.[8] Compared to other organisations that offer similar courses, Karisma is considered superior. Its instructors are usually ITB and UNPAD students and graduates, who are regarded as superior to other students and graduates. The cost of the course is lower than similar courses offered by other organisations. Course participants are required to be members of Karisma and to attend the mentoring program. Parents often prefer their children to attend the *Bimbingan Test* in Salman rather than elsewhere because they believe that besides acquiring general knowledge, their children also learn about Islam. This course attracts many high school students from Bandung and surrounding areas. At first students are only interested in attending the *Bimbingan Test*, but through mentoring gradually they also become attracted to Islam.

Additionally, Karisma often organises other activities to coincide with the Islamic calender, one of the most important being the fasting month *Ramadan*. A special committee, ie. *Panitia Pelaksana Program Ramadhan* (*P3R*, Ramadan Program Organiser Committee) is formed to plan the glorification of the Holy month with various activities. The committee offers various activities, such as *tarawih* and *subuh* sermons, distributing *zakat fithrah*, an Islamic book fair, various courses and trainings, breaking fast (*buka puasa bersama*) with the poor, panel discussions and an art appreciation night. These activities try to accommodate most age groups. These programs also aim to attract other people to come to the mosque, and in turn to become involved in Salman mosque activities or generally in Islamic activities.

As well as the Ramadhan activities there are many activities organised for different age groups. Activities for school and university students are organised by Karisma; for children from primary and secondary schools, Islamic education activities are organised by *PAS (Pembinaan Anak-anak Salman*, Salman Children's Education); Islamic activities among women (*ibu-ibu*) are included in *KKR (Kursus Kesejahteraan Keluarga*, Family Welfare Course); and for the general public there are Sunday morning sermons (*Kuliah Dluha*). In fact, all these activities are usually held on Sunday. Mentoring and PAS activities are held on Sunday morning, starting from 6:00 a.m. Sunday morning sermons are usually held from 8:00 to 10:00. KKR activities are usually held in the afternoon. Every Sunday

---

[8] Completing this course was often regarded as one of the ways to pass the "University Entrance Exam" (*Ujian Masuk Perguruan Tinggi, UMPTN*). Today, when competition to enter higher education has become harder, more and more students are attracted to such courses, although they are quite expensive. Instructors are usually students or graduates of some top universities in Indonesia. The subjects studied in this course are divided into two major areas: mathematics and natural sciences (*Ilmu Pengetahuan Alam, IPA*), such as physics, mathematics, biology, chemistry and social sciences (*Ilmu Pengetahuan Social, IPS*), such as accounting, geography and economics.

Salman Mosque is always crowded by children, adolescents and adults, especially in the morning.

Since its establishment, Salman Mosque has been a model for other Islamic organisations on many university campuses throughout Java and even outside Java. A lecturer of the University of Indonesia told me that in the early 1980s he was part of a group delegated to attend the Islamic course in Salman.[9] Upon their return they applied what they learned at Salman, and became much more involved in Islamic activities on their campus. The mentoring system, which proved effective in Islamic education, has been followed by other Islamic organisations, although they use different names for the approach. The curriculum of Karisma was also used by other organisations. A lecturer of IKIP Surabaya, who was also an organiser of Islamic activities in his campus and for a big Islamic organisation in Surabaya, Al-Falah Foundation (*Yayasan Al-Falah*), explained that the Karisma curriculum forms the Islamic education curriculum on his campus. Similar information was also given by a lecturer at the Andalas University Padang. A group of mosque activists was asked to attend Islamic training at Salman Mosque, and soon after they returned, they applied what they learned.[10] Some Islamic youth organisations from outside Bandung came to Salman to study the Karisma organisational system for managing Islamic activities for young people.

In Bandung, the influence of Salman, and especially Karisma, on other Islamic organisations, both public and university, has been significant. Some university students involved in Salman activities such as LMD and SII training, or in the mentoring program either as participants or as mentors became pioneers of Islamic activities on their university campuses or in their communities. Bambang Pranggono and Toto Tasmara, for example, after their involvement in Salman LMD training later developed Islamic activities at Istiqamah Mosque. Another example is Fahmi, who was involved in Karisma mentoring activities since he was a senior high school student. When he was a student of UNPAD he became a mentor in Karisma, and he was also involved in Islamic activities at UNPAD mosque. Now he is a lecturer at the same university and was nominated as a chief of UNPAD's mosque organisation.

One of the reasons why Karisma became one of the most important campus preaching organisation is that it was the first on-campus Islamic organisation to properly organise -in modern style- various Islamic activities for young people. Moreover, it is supported by a good managerial system and relatively complete facilities. Another reason is that Karisma is strongly associated with the ITB, one of the most prestigious higher education institutes in Bandung and even in

---

[9] Interview, 8 August 1994.
[10] Interview, 7 September 1994.

Indonesia. To a certain degree the prestigious image of ITB became a factor which attracted many young activists to come to the mosque and join Karisma activities.

In the mid-1980s, when there were Islamic activities on almost all large university campuses in Java, the Islamic preaching organisations at some universities began to realise that they should unify in order to make the *Dakwah* movement more effective. At the time the Islamic Campus Preaching Organisations were moving in different directions and operating without coordination. Only a few were in contact with each other. It was felt that if this situation continued, it would disturb the *dakwah* movement generally. A meeting of Islamic Campus Preaching organisations (*Sarasehan Lembaga Dakwah di Kampus*) was held for the first time at Gajah Mada University, Jogjakarta.[11] Delegations from thirteen top universities all over Java attended this meeting.

This meeting was followed by another meeting (see Appendix A), and developed into an annual forum among the university campus preaching organisations. Every year the number of the participants increased, and the scope of the forum became much wider. Since the fifth meeting in IKIP (Teaching and Education Institute) Malang the scope of the forum has been widened to include all of Indonesia. Participants at the meeting not only have come from campus preaching organisation on Javanese university campuses but also from other islands in Indonesia. As well as at this national level, at the regional (province) level such meetings have also been held every year hosted in turn by various universities and academies. In 1994 at both national and regional levels the forum was convened nine times.

Besides unifying various campus preaching organisations throughout Indonesia, the forum also aimed to establish the Islamic preaching organisation in university campuses which did not have one. The forum encourages the members to stimulate and help other universities in their region to establish similar organisations. This is achieved through mutual visitation among activists

---

[11] Four important agreements emerged from this first meeting: 1) to develop an Islamic brotherhood (*Ukhuwah Islamiyah*, Arabic. *Persaudaraan Islam*, Indonesian) amongst Islamic Organisations on university campuses, 2) to meet again in Salman Mosque ITB Bandung in 1987, 3) to reach a mutual understanding among Islamic Organisations on campuses through informal and formal discussion, and 4) to divide the coordination of Islamic preaching organisations on Javanese university campuses (*Lembaga Dakwah Kampus*) into three regions. The west, central and east regions were coordinated respectively by Karisma of ITB, *Jama'ah Shalahuddin* of Gajah Mada University, and the Activity Unit of Islamic Spirituality (Unit Kegiatan Kerohanian Islam UKKI BKK) of Air Langga University.

Later, these regions were named Centres of Regional Communication (PUSKOMWIL, *Pusat Komunikasi Wilayah*). Each large region was divided into two or three smaller regions, coordinated by the Central District Communication (PUSKOMDA, *Pusat Komunikasi Daerah*). The western region, for example, was divided into two: Jabotabek (Jakarta, Bogor, Tanggerang and Bekasi), and Bandung and east Priangan (including Karawang, Sukabumi, Bandung, Sumedang, Tasikmalaya, Ciamis and Cirebon). This division aimed to make easier and more effective communication and coordination amongst university campuses. Through effective coordination, it was hoped that the established Islamic Campus Preaching Organisations could encourage and help those universities which did not have Islamic preaching organisations to develop such organisations.

(individual or collective) of campus preaching organisations in which they share experiences with others that do not have one, encourage, stimulate and help them. Another activity, which became an important element for the development of the campus preaching organisation, is joint activities among those organisations both in regional and national level. These joint activities include Leadership and Management Training, Islamic Teachings Training and Muslim Female Training.

Moreover, the idea to establish Islamic organisations for young people was spread further to other cities and remote areas by the *mudik* (back to home area) tradition of the students. University students, most of whom come from other cities and remote areas in Java and even other islands, go back to their home area during most long holidays. For students involved in Islamic activity, this time is used to form Youth Mosque Associations, or at least an Islamic youth discusion group. They also try to stimulate Islamic activities generally in the areas where they live. However, they often face obstacles in older circles, especially in a community that in ritual aspects is affiliated with NU. The older circles are usually traditional whereas the younger generation is modernist/reformist (see Appendix B).

3.2.2. b. Public Mosques: Mujahidin and Istiqamah

Students involved in Islamic activities began to realise that their activities appeared to be exclusively for university students, and did not touch the wider Muslim community. Consequently, some of them began to extend their activities to public mosques close to their campuses or homes. This awareness forced Bambang Pranggono and Toto Tasmara,[12] two Salman activists, to build another base of Islamic activities for young Muslims in Istiqamah Mosque. Later, this mosque became a centre for young Muslim activists in Bandung to which students, especially senior high school students, came to learn and discuss Islam.

The mosque was built in 1969 by the Istiqamah Foundation, and it was completed and opened for use in 1971. Although Istiqamah Mosque is not affiliated to any Islamic organisation, Istiqamah is regarded as a modernist mosque. This can be seen from the membership of the Istiqamah Foundation board from 1991 to 1995. Most members are important figures of Islamic reformist organisations, namely Muhammadiyah,[13] and Persatuan Islam (PERSIS, Islamic Association).[14]

---

[12] Bambang Pranggono is now a manager of a large real estate firm in Bandung, and is also a preacher. Toto Tasmara is now an employee of a large company in Jakarta.

[13] An Islamic organisation established 18 November 1912 in Kauman Jogjakarta, by Ahmad Dahlan. As an Islamic reformist movement, Muhammadiyah emphasised its program of (1) purifying Islam from the incorrect teachings, (2) reformation of Islamic education, (3) reformation of Islamic thought and (4) defending Islam from Western influence and Christian teachings (Natsir 1972:16). These programs are implemented in religious, educational and social activities. Besides religious reformation, Muhammadiyah established various social institutions such as hospitals and orphanages. Muhammadiyah also established schools and other educational institutions as a response to the establishment of Dutch schools, believed to be a means of promoting the Christian mission (Poerbakawatja 1970:22).

[14] PERSIS is an Islamic mass organisation like Muhammadiyah, which was established in Bandung 12 September 1923. It was a response to the predicament of Indonesian Muslims, who, in the view of this

Board members include K.H. Hambali Ahmad, a well-known Muhammadiyah *ulama* in Bandung, and K.H. Rusyad Nurdin, one of the PERSIS *ulama*. The pattern of Islamic thought within this mosque is reformist and modernist, and because of this, all subjects preached should be in accordance with the above patterns of Islamic thought, and all the preachers should be those who come from the modernist or reformist circles.

At each prayer time, many people come to pray (*shalat*), including high school students waiting for their classes to begin. During prayer time on Fridays, the mosque is always crowded, and indeed the mosque cannot always accommodate them, many of them having to pray outside. During the month of Ramadhan, as in university mosques, the mosque organises various special activities, such as religious sermons, Islamic training for school students, Islamic courses for women, preaching courses, panel discussions and organising alms (*zakat*). Such activities are organised by the board of the Istiqamah Foundation. However, the practical organisers of these activities are usually young activists.

The involvement of young Muslim activists, according to K.H. Rusyad Nurdin, started with the establishment of the mosque in 1971. At that stage young Muslim activists had not been included in the organisational structure of the Istiqamah Foundation. Moreover there were no special activities for young Muslim activists. They only participated in the general mosque activities. Islamic activities for young Muslim activists in Istiqamah developed during the mid-1970s, when a few Salman Mosque activists, most of them ITB students, began to organise special activities for school students and young Muslim activists. These started with an informal, small-group discussion program, usually conducted after Sunday morning sermons. At that time, according to an informant, such activities had no name. The number of participants gradually increased, especially among the young. It was at this stage that the idea emerged among activists to establish a special section within the mosque's organisational structure to organise Islamic activities for young Muslims.

After Islamic activities for young people were established in this mosque, the idea emerged to extend such an organisation and its activities to other mosques in other cities. To achieve this goal, Toto Tasmara proposed an idea to establish an organisation in which youth organisations of various mosques could assemble. This goal was achieved in Ramadhan 1976, when delegations from Surabaya, Yogyakarta, Jakarta and Bandung gathered in Istiqamah Mosque. With the approval of the Indonesian Council of Religious Clergy (*MUI, Majelis Ulama Indonesia*), an organisation called the Communication Body for Mosque Youth

organisation, were trapped into "stagnation (*jumud*), superstition (*Churafat* and *Tahayyul*), heresy (*Bid'ah*), polytheism (*Syirik*), and ... Christian Dutch Colonialism". See *Tafsir Qanun Asasi Persatuan Islam*. Panitia Perubahan Qanun Asasi Persatuan Islam. Bandung: Pusat Pimpinan Persatuan Islam, Muktamar Persatuan Islam VIII, 1967)

of Indonesia (*Badan Komunikasi Pemuda Masjid Indonesia*, BKPMI) was established. The first leader of this organisation was Toto Tasmara. The main aim of this organisation was to make use of mosques not only for ritual activities, but also for the quality development of the Islamic community (*umat Islam*) and nation (*bangsa* Indonesia). It was felt that mosques should become a centre for youth activities in the widest sense. Moreover, mosques, through various activities, were seen as being able to balance secular influences on the young generation (BKPMI 1991:1). The popular slogan of this organisation was "Back to the mosque" (Tempo, 13.5.1989).

To achieve their aims, BKPMI tried to intensify communication, consultation and synchronisation of mosque youth organisations throughout Indonesia. For established organisations, BKPMI provided clear directions and aims for the organisations and their activities. For mosques which did not have such an organisation, BKPMI assisted and encouraged the younger generations and mosque boards to establish them. To support these activities, various programs were introduced, including magazine publications, joint activities amongst mosque youth organisations, Islamic education and various other courses, and Al-Quran Kindergarten. Every three years BKPMI held a national meeting to share experiences to decide on national programs and to choose a new board. By 1992 such meetings had been held four times. Today, BKPMI has spread to all provinces of Indonesia.

In the late 1970s and early 1980s, Islamic activities among youngsters in Istiqamah developed further. Many more school and university students from the Bandung area came to this mosque to attend sermons, and to discuss and learn about Islam. Some informants, who lived about 15 kilometres away from the Istiqamah Mosque, said that they woke up before dawn so that they could arrive at the mosque on time and attend the sermon. This was quite extraordinary, because public mosques are usually attended by the community in which the mosque is located. The attractiveness of Istiqamah Mosque was, perhaps, influenced by the emergence of the *Jama'ah Imran* (Imran Group),[15] which made Istiqamah Mosque a centre of its activities.

Jama'ah Imran attracted young Muslim activists for several reasons. The appearance of its leader, Imran, who was dynamic, radical and attractive, and his preachings, which were critical, were important factors in the recruitment

---

[15] The Jama'ah Imran movement was an Islamic movement lead by Imran Muhammad Zein, who had previously been unemployed, stubborn, fond of gambling, drunk and fighting. Because of this, he had been in jail, although for a short time. Furthermore, his father had said "I cannot stand it anymore. You or I should leave Medan". Imran replied, "Let me go". Not long after this, in 1972, he went to Saudi Arabia. His real motivation was not clear; whether he wanted to confess or to look for a job. Imran admitted that "In Saudi Arabia he found what he was looking for in Islam, safety and happiness". With his young Indonesian friends, Imran planned that when they returned to Indonesia, they would establish an Islamic group (*Jama'ah*) which would apply Islam as revealed in the Qur'an and Sunnah (Tradition of the Prophet) (Any 1982:21).

process of this movement. From his preaching held every Sunday morning, it was clear that he rejected Pancasila as being superior to Islam. Such an idea at that time in government eyes was a considerable offense. Later Imran also criticised Indonesian Islamic figures, such as Natsir, Hamka, Idham Khalid and E.Z. Muttaqin, who were respectively the leader of Masyumi, the leader of Indonesian Muslim Clergy Assembly (MUI, *Majlis Ulama Indonesia*), the leader of Nahdlatul Ulama and the leader of West Java region MUI, for not struggling (*berjuang*) for Islam. They, in Imran's view, only struggled for "their stomach" (Any 1982:16). Such ideas, of course, provoked conflict not only within the Istiqamah circle but also in the wider Muslim community. Opposition to this movement became even clearer when it became involved in terrorist activities, such as robbery, hijacking and murder.[16] In August 1980 Istiqamah Mosque was raided by the army and police, and forty-four young activists were arrested initially. In the following days more activists were arrested.

This event led to a decline in the number of young Muslim activists attending the mosque. Many were scared to come to the mosque because they did not want to be accused of being a member of the Imran movement. Furthermore, parents of activists forbade their children attending the mosque. More widely, it created a phobia in the Muslim community about being involved in Islamic activities. However, after a year-long period of stagnation, Muslim youth activities in Istiqamah started to re-emerge. Students, mostly school students, again began to attend Sunday morning sermons. Some Istiqamah activists, who were not involved in the Imran case, began to reorganise Islamic activities for young Muslim activists. In the mid-1980s, Istiqamah again became a centre of Islamic activities among young people. At this time, the motor of Islamic activities, as discussed later, comprised those students involved in various Islamic groups (*harakahs*).

There is another important mosque which serves as a centre for young Muslim activists in Bandung: Mujahidin Mosque. It is located in the inner city, about two kilometres from the city centre (*Alun-alun*). It is surrounded by a dense population, by schools, a market, sports fields and busy roads. There are at least ten junior and senior high schools close to the mosque. Each prayer session, especially noon and afternoon sessions, are crowded by students. Moreover, some schools organise praying lessons in this mosque. According to research organised by IKIP Bandung, almost 75 percent of those attending daily and Friday prayer sessions are young people (Djamari 1988:71).

---

[16] In his trial, Imran explained that his idea to take up arms (*angkat senjata*) was inspired by Anderson's book about the President and a copy of a CSIS document about a meeting between Dewan Gereja Indonesia (DGI) and MAWI, signed by Ali Murtopo, T.B. Simatupang and others. In the latter, he found that there was an attempt from Christian groups to eliminate Indonesian Muslims. In Imran's view "if someone wants to crush me, I will crush him first. And if there are people who want to crush the Muslim *umat*, the Muslim *umat* should move and crush them first".

Building of the mosque began in 1955 when a mosque development committee, which consisted of Masyumi figures, was allotted an area by the local government. In the same year, the project was assigned to the Muhammadiyah organisation which has administered it ever since. Mujahidin Mosque began as a temporary mosque, and the building proceeded gradually and was completed in 1993. Throughout the building process, the mosque was used as a proper mosque, for daily prayers, Friday prayer and sermons.

Unlike Istiqamah Mosque, the Mujahidin Mosque is clearly affiliated with Muhammadiyah. As a consequence, all its policies and activities are in accordance with Muhammadiyah policy. Sermons must be in agreement with the Muhammadiyah teaching guidelines. All preachers, either as *khatib* (speaker) during Friday prayers or as speakers during regular sermons are from modernist organisations, such as Muhammadiyah and PERSIS. Islamic activities among young activists in Mujahidin mosque have developed since the mid-1970s, when some university students from various higher education organisations and high schools in Bandung began to gather and discuss Islam informally. It started when young people who attended regular sermons at the Mosque got to know each other and began small discussions.

In the early 1980s, Islamic youth activities in Mujahidin mosque developed further, and the number of young Muslim activists increased, especially when young Muslim activists who had always attended Istiqamah Mosque moved to Mujahidin mosque because of the Imran case. Beside being involved in general mosque activities, they organised gatherings, mosque camps and short Islamic training courses. During these activities some speakers addressed Islamic subjects such as the Meaning of Islam, basic faith (*Aqidah*) and *Jihad* (Holy War). A subject always mentioned was Muslim community problems (*Problematika Umat Islam*). According to an informant, almost all speakers (all university students) were very critical of the government. Moreover, they believed that Islam in Indonesia was being forced into a corner (*dipojokkan*). The latter idea was often spread through youth secretly distributing pamphlets to university and school campuses. University students from various universities in Bandung area organised these activities for senior high school students and taught them Islam. University students visited the senior high schools from which they had graduated to recruit students.

These two mosques are quite similar. First, they are located in urban[17] areas close to universities and other educational organisations. Sociologically Islam in urban areas has been dominated, as Fachry Ali puts it, by Islamic reformists,

[17] The urban environment with its characteristics of "isolation, insecurity and loneliness" as a result of "loosening of traditional social bonds... [and] less apt to develop close personal association" (Louis Wirth and George Simmel in Curran and Renzetti 1990:579) seem to be a fertile field for the development of the Islamic movement.

such as Muhammadiyah and PERSIS. This has led to another similarity: in terms of their religious views, they are modernist mosques. In addition, these two mosques show that the Islamic resurgence movements among young people are mostly developed in Islamic reformist and modernist environments. Although in Bandung there are some big mosques organised by NU,[18] to date I have not identified centres of Islamic youth activities among the mosques organised by traditional Muslim Nahdlatul Ulama. These similarities show that there is a clear connection between the reformist/modernist and the current Islamic resurgence among young people. There is a continuation of ideas that previously raised by the modernist and reformist movements that emerged since the turn of the century.

3.2.3. c. *Harakah*: Independent Movements

Harakah is an Arabic word meaning 'movement' and refers specifically to Islamic movements. However, *harakah* does not refer to conventional Islamic movements, such as *Nahdlatul Ulama* (Association of Muslim Scholar, NU), Muhammadiyah, PERSIS (Persatuan Islam, Islamic unity) or other Muslim organisations. Neither does it refer to formal[19] *dakwah* activities held by campus preaching organisations such as at Salman Mosque of ITB, Jama'ah Shalahuddin of Gajah Mada University in Jogjakarta and other Islamic organisations on university campuses which are officially approved by universities. The term *harakah* emerged and has developed since the early 1980s along with the further development of Islamic activities among young people on university campuses and public mosques. According to figures from one *harakah*, there are about ten *harakah* spread over many campuses and public mosques throughout large cities of Indonesia, including Bandung. A few reported by *Tempo* in 1993 included *Ikhwan al-Muslimun* (Muslim Brotherhood), *Hizb al-Tahrir* (Liberation Party), *Tarbiyah* (Education), *Salafiyah, Dar al-Arqam*, and *Jama'ah Tabligh*. All of these movements arose outside Indonesia, most coming from the Middle East (*Tempo* 3.4.1993).

Harakah, in a broad sense, are organised Islamic movements[20] aimed at applying Islam comprehensively in all aspects of life, as the Prophet Muhammad exemplified. On the basis of the Qur'an and *Sunnah* (the words, behaviour and

---

[18] There has traditionally been a division between modernist and conservative among Indonesian Muslims. In the 1950s Islamic political power was divided between the reformist Masyumi and conservative NU. All Islamic reformist, modernist and even fundamentalist groups affiliated with the former, whereas other Islamic conservative groups affiliated with the latter (Feith 1982:218).

[19] The word 'formal' in 'formal Islamic activities' or 'formal Islamic movement' means that those activities or movements are approved officially by authorities. The world 'informal' indicates the contrary. Campus Islamic preaching institutions and public mosques are formal organisations because they are approved by the government or by the universities.

[20] According to Kalim Siddiqui in his book *The Islamic Movement: a system approach*, "The Islamic movement is a world wide, open, diffuse system in which individual Muslims or Muslims organised in groups are consciously working towards the reconsolidation of the Ummah into a behavioural, operational and a goal seeking system" (1980:9).

pattern of life of the Prophet), they seek to establish concrete Islamic alternatives to existing socio-economic and political organisations in Muslim countries which are believed to depart from Islam. They seek to resurrect the glory of Islam as achieved during the era of the Prophet and his companions. This idea stems from a deep consciousness that the world's Muslim community (*Ummah*) is in a state of decline. They believe that most Muslim countries -whether ruled by Islamic governments or not- are politically, economically, socially and culturally under non-Islamic foreign (Western: Europe and America, and Soviet) domination. Muslim countries, all of which are 'third world countries', are closely linked with poverty, backwardness and dependence on foreign loans. Some leaders of a few rich Muslim countries have been the 'arms' and 'puppets' of foreign powers, which often suppress any Islamic movements. Moreover, in their view moral decadence is a common trend throughout Muslim countries. Like Sayyid Qutb, they found that:

> Now [Muslims] are in a *jahiliyah* (ignorance) period, like in the early period of Islam or even worse. Everything that exists around us is *jahiliyah*, including conception, beliefs, customs, traditions, sources of science, art and literature, laws and constitutions. Many things that we thought of as Islamic cultures, Islamic sources, and Islamic ideas, are in fact the product of *jahiliyah* (1978:1st chapter).

Although these *harakah* have similar ideological views each has different interpretations about what real problems are faced by the Ummah. These differences have resulted in various types of Islamic groups, with each harakah stressing a specific problem and a specific solution.

Those *harakah* reported by Tempo are all imported *harakah*, which developed later. In fact, local Islamic movements in Bandung emerged in the mid-1970s, when some militant Muslim groups organised underground Islamic movements. These Islamic movements originally reflected local backgrounds, environments, ideas and other factors, although they were inevitably influenced by imported Islamic movements. In Bandung, there are at least two important Islamic movements which developed among, and greatly influenced, young Muslim activists. These movements are the Young/New DI (*Darul Islam Muda/Baru*) and LP3K (*Lembaga Pembinaan dan Pengembangan Pesantren Kilat*, Institute for Education and Development of Islamic Short Course Training). Among the movement activists, they are called respectively IIN, reversal of NII (*Negara Islam Indonesia*, Indonesian Islamic State), and PK (Pesantren Kilat). I have not included *Jama'ah* Imran here because it lasted only a very short time, emerging in late 1979 and dissolving in 1980. Moreover it did not influence greatly the development of Islamic movements, either in Bandung or more generally in Indonesia.

The Young DI is a term I use to refer to various movements which are historically and ideologically related to a 1950s Islamic rebel movement. It is difficult to identify each of these Young DI movements, because although they have similar historical and ideological sources, they have different names and different teachings. This is, perhaps, understandable given that the important figures or the founders of movements are those members of the *Darul Islam* (DI) movement, who scattered and hid in various places in Indonesia. They continue to share their ideas with the people, especially with young people in the community where they live. To avoid the suspicion of the authorities, and to adapt to the social and political environment, they have modified their teachings and identities.

The basic idea of this movement can be traced to the establishment of the *Darul Islam* itself. According to Van Nieuwenhujijze (cited in Boland 1985:59), Kartosuwirjo (full name Sekarmadji Maridjan Kartosuwirjo) began openly preaching about the idea of an Islamic State in the Malangbong Garut region, about 30 kilometres east of Bandung, in 1935. On 14 August 1945, according to Alers (in Boland 1985:60), Kartosuwirjo proclaimed an independent Islamic state, but when Sukarno and Hatta proclaimed Indonesian independence on 17th August 1945, he took the side of the Indonesian Republic. However, it did not last long because he rejected any negotiations between the government and the Dutch. On 7 August 1949, Kartosuwirjo proclaimed for the second time an Indonesian Islamic State (*Negara Islam Indonesia*)[21], and proclaimed himself as the head (*Imam*) of the new state, which was better known as *Darul Islam* (territory or house of Islam). The law of the state was Islamic law, and the state constitution was called Kanun Azasy (in Arabic, *Qanun al-Asasi*). These documents argued that Islamic law should be adhered to by all Muslims, whereas non-Muslims were free to practise their religions.

All members of the Young DI movements believe that the Indonesian Islamic State has continued to exist since the time it was declared in 1949. According to this movement there are only two states: the Islamic state (*Dar al-Islam*) and the infidel state (*Dar al-Harb*). Each person has to choose between the two. The present regime is considered to be a *kafir* (infidel) regime as it opposes the Islamic state. Moreover, according to one informant, the Indonesian Republic has seized the Islamic state, and there are continual confrontations between these two states. There is a tendency to regard other Muslims who are not members of the Young DI groups, as being un-Islamic, if not infidel. In the late 1980s, for example, some Young DI activists in Istiqamah mosque and in UNPAD Jatinangor Mosques, stole donation boxes (*kotak amal*) from the mosques, because they believed such

---

[21] Its proclamation text is "In the name of Allah the Compassionate and the Merciful, we the Muslim community (*Umat Islam*) of Indonesian people hereby declare the establishment of the Indonesian Islamic State. The law of the Indonesian Islamic State is Islamic law. God is Great, God is Great, God is Great".

acts were *fa'i* (robbing the enemy, in a war situation in the early era of the Prophet). Some groups of the Young DI also forbade watching TV and listening to the radio, because they believed it would "damage" their morality.

Similar to the "old DI" in the period of Kartosuwirjo, the Young DI tried to spread the idea of establishing an Indonesian Islamic State by appealing to the Muslim community in public mosques, university campuses, schools and other places, through various activities. As in public mosques and university campuses, they also held gatherings, religious sermons, short Islamic courses, and sports or military simulation training. All of these activities were organised secretly and carefully, and were to be attended only by members. Such care was taken because they believed that if the authorities knew about the activities and their involvement in them, they would be jailed. During the gatherings, besides learning about and discussing Islam, they also discussed contemporary political matters.

A distinctive activity of Young DI movements was *bai'ah* or an oath of allegiance ceremony for new members, usually presided over by the leader (*Imam*) of the Indonesian Islamic State. The ceremony began with recitation from the Qur'an, and with the *Imam* giving a short speech. The *bai'ah* began with the leader saying the *shahadat*, "There is no God but Allah, and the Prophet Muhammad is His messenger". This was followed by a statement that they would obey the constitution and rules of the Indonesian Islamic State. Unlike other *harakah*, as we shall see later, there was no special training before the *bai'ah* process. Recruitment took place only through personal approach. People with similar views about Islam would be asked to attend some of the gatherings, and then they would be asked to perform *bai'ah*. Such open recruitment made it easy for the authorities to infiltrate, and in the early 1990s almost all of the important figures of the movement were arrested and sentenced. However, this did not mean that the movement died completely because other members continued to spread their ideas.

Another important local Islamic movement was LP3K, more commonly known as the *Pesantren Kilat* movement. According to Mursalin Dahlan (1994), the founder of the movement, the thrust of the Pesantren Kilat was to "defend the basic faith (*aqidah*) of young Muslim generations, especially school and university students from secularisation movements and the Christian Mission." He further referred to the struggle of *santri* against Dutch and Japanese colonialism. Thus to resist secularisation and the Christian mission it was necessary to create *santri*, and *pesantren* were needed to educate *santri*. Therefore, in 1976 Mursalin Dahlan established an organisation called Pesantren Kilat (Islamic Short Course Training). Since that time, Pesantren Kilat has become an Islamic movement which tries to revive the comprehensive teachings of Islam (*Kaffah*)[22] among Muslim community, especially the younger generations.

To further build and develop the Pesantren Kilat, Mursalin Dahlan in the same year established the Organisation for the Building and Development of Pesantren Kilat (*Lembaga Pembinaan dan Pengembangan Pesantren Kilat, LP3K*). Through continuous and aggressive propagation this movement developed rapidly. In the early 1980s the network of *Pesantren Kilat* spread to other big cities throughout Java, while the centre of the movement remained in Bandung. Activities of the movement were usually based in the premises (such as house, sport hall, musholla) of members of the movement. They sometimes used public mosques, university campuses, school campuses and other places, after they managed to disguise themselves to get approval from the owner. For important meetings and special training, they usually used facilities provided by members, eg. houses, sports halls, or other buildings.

The term Pesantren Kilat has a special meaning which indicates the types of activities of the movement. Pesantren are Islamic schools to educate young Muslims to become *Ulama* (Islamic scholar). Students (*santri*) usually spend five to ten years in mastering Islamic teachings, and when they graduate from the pesantren they become *ustadz* (Islamic teacher) or ulama. The word 'kilat', means flash of lightning. These meanings taken together show that *Pesantren Kilat* is an Islamic school aimed at creating Islamic scholars and Islamic proselytisers in a very short time.

Pesantren Kilat as an activity was a short Islamic course or training, in which about five to ten participants, most of them school and university students, study Islamic teachings and the problems of the Muslim community. The course lasted three or four days, usually starting on Friday afternoon and finishing on Monday morning. During the course participants were isolated from the outside world; they did not read newspapers, listen to the radio, watch TV or have contact with people outside the house. They spent all of their three or four days in the same house, with the same people. The idea to create a condition of isolation with less than ten participants, according to Dahlan, derived from the story of the *ashab al-kahf* (people of the cave) in chapter 18 of the Quran, The Cave. It relates how seven young, devout believers escaped from the tyranny of injustice, and hid in a cave. In the cave they could not see or hear anything; they were completely isolated from the outside world.[23]

---

[22] An Arabic word meaning 'comprehensive'. The idea was taken from the 208th verse of the 2nd chapter of the Qur'an.

[23] In Christian tradition it was known as the legend of the Seven Sleepers of the Ephesus. The story in Christianity and Islam is quite similar, with the differences perhaps in its spiritual lessons. In *The Decline and Fall of the Roman Empire*, as cited by Abdullah Yusuf' Ali in *The Meaning of The Holy Qur'an*, it was told that in the era of Roman Emperor when Christians were persecuted, seven Christian youths of Ephesus escaped and hid themselves in a cave in a mountain from the oppressive tyrant, Decius.

Throughout the course, participants engaged in two kinds of activities, core and supportive activities. The former were sermons and discussions, whereas the latter included reciting the Qur'an, praying *tahajud* (midnight optional prayer) and daily prayers. Participants woke very early, at about 3:00 a.m., to pray *tahajud* and to recite the Qur'an. At about 4:00 a.m. they attended morning prayer, which was followed by a short speech, the speaker usually being one of the participants. From 5:00 to 8:00 a.m. participants attended a sermon followed by a discussion. After the sermon participants rested, bathed and then ate together. The food was usually put in a big container from which two groups of participants ate together with their fingers. The food was prepared by the organisers, and was purchased using financial contributions from the participants and the organisers. By about 9.30 a.m., participants were ready to listen to another speech and discussion, which finished in time for the noon prayer. After the noon prayer, lunch and a short rest, at 1.30 p.m. another speaker was ready to give a speech, finishing before the afternoon prayer. The afternoon prayer completed, participants had a short rest or walked around inside the room before attending another sermon. Participants took a bath, had dinner and then performed the evening (*maghrib*) prayer, read the Qur'an and rested before the last session of the day, 8:00– 10.00 p.m.. At 10:00 p.m., participants were asked to sleep, and were woken at 3:00 a.m.. On the last night, Pesantren Kilat activities were brought to a close by an important ceremony. This began with a short period of self-reflection and self-introspection led by an instructor: one by one participants came forward and did *bai'ah* (oath) by saying the *shahadat* (the profession of faith: "There is no God except Allah, and the Prophet Muhammad is His messenger") and shaking hands with the instructor, usually the leader of the movement or a senior member of the movement.[24] After this, one of the organisers gave an Islamic or Arabic name to each participant who did not already have one. However, in some cases, as an informant said, although participants already had Islamic names, they also were given new Islamic names. These new names were later used among the members of the movement. Sometimes these new names were used even in daily social life, because the recipients believed that their new names were much better and imparted a new personality.

The Pesantren Kilat activity was organised by a committee consisting of university and school students, all of whom were members of the movement. Usually, participants who completed the Pesantren Kilat activity were asked to organise similar activities in the following months or even in the same month. Participants were also encouraged to recruit their friends at school, their

They slept, and continued to sleep for some generations and even centuries. When they awoke, they thought that they were still in the same period. However, when one of them came to the town, he realised that the world had changed. The Christian religion had become the state religion (Ali 1991:709).

[24] This ceremony is very much the same with the conversion ceremony when a non-Muslim converts to Islam. One informant says, "After that ceremony I found myself as a 'real' Muslim. Before hand my Islam was only hereditary (*keturunan*) without understanding and consciousness".

neighbours and even their brothers and sisters to attend Pesantren Kilat. Such high mobility contributed to the movement spreading widely and rapidly.

The instructors of the Pesantren Kilat were the founder himself and alumni of the Pesantren Kilat. Their levels of education varied: some were senior high school students or university students, and others were university graduates. They were all members of the movement who had received special instructor training. No outsiders, even *ulama* and Muslim intellectuals, were ever invited to be instructors in Pesantren Kilat activities. Each instructor usually mastered one special subject of the Pesantren Kilat syllabus, and could be called upon at any time to give a speech on that subject.

Activities of the Pesantren Kilat movement were interrupted in 1983, when some of its members became involved in subversive and terrorist activities. Authorities accused the LP3K movement of being a "training ground for militant cadres prepared to set up an Indonesian Islamic State or NII". A leader of the Surabaya LP3K, who was also a preacher, was charged with subversion and was sentenced to twenty years, because of his preachings. Another member of LP3K was sentenced to twelve years for his involvement in distributing illegal pamphlets. Further, some members of LP3K were accused of being involved in a series of bombing incidents in Jakarta, Malang, Yogyakarta and Surabaya. One member of LP3K was accused of being involved in LP3K courses, in a series of bombings, and even in a plot to assassinate Suharto, and was sentenced to life imprisonment. The 1985 and 1986 trials of many subversive and terrorist cases involving Islamic groups showed that the LP3K network had relations with a range of opposition powers, such as the Petition-of-50 group.

From 1983, the level of activity of the LP3K movement began to decline, until finally it ceased to function in the mid-1980s. However, wherever they are, alumni of the Pesantren Kilat continue to spread ideas learned in Pesantren Kilat. The term "Pesantren Kilat" and its type of activity has been used by various Islamic organisations in recent development. It became a fashionable type of Islamic education in Indonesia, usually held during holiday times, especially during the month of Ramadhan. Some government offices, big companies and other organisations held such activities, either for the children of the employees or for the employees themselves.

Some members of the Pesantren Kilat movement moved to and became involved in other *harakah*, which began to develop in 1982 and 1983, when the Pesantren Kilat movement had begun to decline. Some other members of the movement developed a new movement with a new orientation, new strategy, new style of education and a new name. In terms of ideology, however, the new movement was similar to its predecessor. Its type of educational process was modified and divided into three stages: *Ula* (first), *Wustho* (second) and *A'la* (high). Each of these stages had special follow-up activities involving what were called *usrah* groups, which had a core group of five to ten persons led by one of its members called *naqib* (leader). *Usrah* group meetings were held weekly or fortnightly at members' houses in turn. The gatherings usually lasted from Saturday night to Sunday morning, and on Sunday morning, together with other members of the movement, the group often engaged in sporting activities such as football, badminton and occasionally swimming.

During *usrah* gatherings, commitment of the members to the movement was reinforced and strengthened. Meetings started with reciting the Qur'an and checking each others' memories of verses of the Qur'an. An instructor (*zaim*) who had completed the higher stages of training gave a speech on a planned Islamic subject and this was followed by a discussion. After this, members of the group discussed topics such as the current socio-political situation or the personal problems of members, and finally they mutually advised one another (*taushiyah*, an Arabic term, meaning 'mutual teaching'). The gatherings finished at about 10:00 p.m., and at 3:00 a.m. participants woke up to pray *tahajud*. One important aim of these activities was to increase a sense of brotherhood among members. Such activities did have this sort of significance for many, especially for university students, most of whom were far from their families.

Although not identical, *usrah*-type activities were in fact used by various *harakah* which developed on university campuses. This type of activity, as in the development of Islamic revivalism in Malaysia, was "the most effective vehicle" in spreading the ideas of the Islamic movement (Anwar 1987: 45). The term *usrah*, used to describe a type of Islamic education group, can be traced back to the Muslim Brotherhood (*Ikhwan al-Muslimun*) movement in Egypt. According to Hassan al-Banna, the founder and the leader of the movement, *usrah* is a family, which bound Muslims into brotherhood on the basis of Islam. There are three pillars of *usrah*, namely acquaintance (*ta'aruf*), mutual understanding (*tafahum*) and mutual responsibility (*takaful*) (al-Banna 1979:4–10).

During the mid to late 1980s, the number of *harakah* that developed amongst young Muslim activists increased. *Harakah* which developed during this period, in addition to local Islamic movements, mostly came from outside Indonesia, especially from the Middle East. These movements, as I mentioned before, were *Ikhwan al-Muslimin*, *Hizb al-Tahrir*, *Tarbiyah*, *Salafiyah*, *Dar al-Arqam*, and *Jama'ah Tabligh* (see Appendix C).

These Islamic groups because of their independent characteristics and their aggressive attempt to recruit and train the followers were an important channel by which Islamic resurgence ideas spread rapidly among young Muslim activists. The radical, rebellious, underground and secretive nature of these Islamic groups became important factors which attracted young activists to join them. Members of these groups usually became activists and the motor of various Islamic activities both in campus preaching organisation and in the public mosques, through which they recruited their new members. This does not mean that there is a clear division among activists of Islamic groups, preaching organisations and of public mosques, since one activist can be a member of an Islamic group and at the same time an activist of public mosque and of preaching organisation.

3.3 Fertile Milieu

This Islamic resurgence could not take place successfully without the right social and political conditions. How much then do the conditions of the early resurgence still apply?

One of the most common phenomena associated with the development of the Islamic revival among young Muslims was the increased number of young female Muslims who wore *Jilbab*.[25] Since 1977, a few female Salman activists had begun to wear *jilbab*, and gradually this practice spread widely amongst young, female Muslim activists, especially university and school students. Wearing this type of cloth spread through various Islamic trainings activities. Among the *harakah* and Islamic movements generally, according to a leader of one *harakah* in Bandung, wearing a *jilbab* became one of the parameters of success of training or organised activity. If female participants continued to wear *jilbab* after the training it meant that the training had been successful.

In 1982 when many more students were wearing *jilbab*, even when they went to their schools, the Ministry of Education and Culture created a new act concerning student uniforms. It detailed acceptable uniforms for both male and female students. The act forbade female students to wear *jilbab* within the school area. As a consequence, those who wore *jilbab* had to choose between removing their *jilbab* and moving to other schools which allowed them to wear such clothes.[26]

---

[25] Garmen for women which reveals only the face, and falls down loosely to below the chest or the waist.

[26] Such a case first occurred in one of the top senior high schools in Bandung, namely SMA 3 (Sekolah Menengah Atas Negeri 3 Bandung). In 1982 a sports teacher forbade some female students from wearing tracksuits. The teacher said that if they did not wear short pants, he would mark them down. Moreover, although they came to school, they were not allowed to enter the classroom nor to attend the class. In later developments, they were not allowed even to enter the school area. However, the school staff did not expel them formally from the school. Students felt that they were being treated discriminatively, and asked the *ulama*, for their support, but the *ulama* could not do much. The students also went to the Regional House of Representatives asking for a clear legal explanation of the prohibition to wearing *jilbab*. Similar cases also occurred in other state public schools in Bandung, and other places throughout Java.

Various negotiations were held among students, parents, *ulama*, and government authorities. In general there were two sides, and these were in confrontation: the government authorities and the students. The government authorities insisted that they only did what the Act and their superiors asked them to do. Moreover, according to the government authorities, *jilbab* or *kerudung* was not a religious matter. This led to the accusations that the spread of such clothing was only a political device of certain interests, the identity and nature of whom was not clear. In contrast, students believed that they wore *jilbab* for religious reasons.[26] They argued that they knew nothing about politics. Furthermore, they argued that what they did was guaranteed by the Indonesian Constitution (Undang-Undang Dasar 1945), which

This led to a "confrontation" between students and the government. Such confrontation created and reinforced two attitudes among students and young Muslims activists generally. First, suspicious responses from the government created a new view that the government was actually not in favour of Islam. For student and Muslim activists who already viewed the present regime as un-Islamic, government actions reinforced their belief. Second, the lack of comment by the *ulama*, who were unable to advocate the freedom of using veils, to a certain degree created an antipathy toward *ulama* among young Muslim activists. Furthermore, the feeling of powerlessness and hopelessness of the overwhelming majority of Muslims led to frustration and alienation. Such feelings, given that Muslims are in the majority, were described by Wertheim (1986) as a "Majority with minority mentality".

Another influential event was the Tanjung Priok massacre in 1984, followed by a series of trials of many Islamic activists, throughout Java. The beginning of the first case was a Tanjung Priok massacre in which hundreds of people (Muslim) were killed. A similar massacre against Muslims occurred in 1989, when an army operation was held to quell unrest (Tapol 92:4:89) and 'suspicious' Islamic activities (Tempo 18:4:1989) in the Lampung province. According to one source, hundreds of people were killed and others injured. These massacres were followed by many arrests and trials of the Muslim activists. For Muslim activists, these cases showed that the government continously oppressed Islam.

These various cases from the late 1970s to the late 1980s illustrate some important points. First, there was a clear indication that government authorities were cautious and suspicious about the new tendency among young Muslims. This cautiousness often was marked by unsympathetic and even oppressive attitudes such as the prohibition to use veils that identified them as political devices. Second, government attitudes in turn led to a state of frustration and antipathy towards the government; fertile conditions for the development of the Islamic movement because the teachings and methods of the Islamic resurgence movement provided a kind of shelter from that frustration. At this point, I agree with Emerson (1981), who says "Religion is like a nail. The harder you hit it, the deeper it goes into the wood". Here, some conditions of the early emergence in early 1970s ie. frustration and dissatisfactions still apply in this development

says that all citizens are free to perform religious rituals, appropriate to their religion. In addition, they pointed out that they never made trouble or did anything wrong at their schools, and they were never involved in any political group. In fact, according to the *Panji Masyarkat* report, many of them performed at the top of their class.

While negotiations continued, application of the uniform act continued. All attempts at negotiation seemed to come to a dead end. Finally, in 1984 and 1985, almost all female students who wore *jilbab* moved to other schools which allowed their female students to wear *jilbab*, whereas some others remained in the same school, for examination reason, but took off their veils when they entered the campus area. In Bandung, most of those who were expelled from their school because of their veils, moved to a private school namely PGII (Persatuan Guru Islam Indonesia, Indonesian Islamic Teachers Association).

stage. The difference is that in this stage the spread of the frustration and dissatisfaction became much more pervasive, since it spread through various channels.

To conclude there are some distinct characteristics of this development stage. First, the movement initially centered on charismatic figures but developed with the establishment of various organisations, both formal and informal, through which the resurgent ideas dispersed effectively. Another important characteristic of this stage was the aggressive preaching and evangelical attempts launched by those organisations. Finally, as in the first stage the common trend during the stage was towards emotional and radical expression.

Chapter 4: Routinisation of the Movement: Impacts of Social and Political Changes

4.1 Introduction

In Ramadan 1994, I went to Jakarta to get my visa from the Australian Embassy. When the time for afternoon prayer came, I went to the *Musholla*[1] of a private bank, located in the basement of a car park. I was struck by the scene there. The basement usually used for a car park was crowded by approximately 800 people. Men and women, most of them employees of the bank, were sitting on plastic mats waiting for the afternoon (*zhuhur*) prayer. There were rows of men at the front and women at the back. In between the men and the women was a green curtain about one meter high. (On Fridays at this *musholla*, however, women do not pray at the same time as men). After praying, a bank employee gave a fluent Arabic introduction, announcing the speaker for that day, Imaduddin Abdurrahim. After Imaduddin's sermon, all employees returned to their offices and resumed working. According to the bank employee beside me, this activity had been conducted every day since the first day of Ramadan in 1994.

This quite new activity emerged only during the 1990s, and is only one phenomenon in a new wave of religious consciousness among the Indonesian Muslim middle class, and Indonesian Muslims in general. Along with the emergence of this new wave there have been some changes in social, political and economic life. These changes, according to Indonesian and foreign observers, are the result of the relation between the government and Islam, which has become much more intimate. This new wave cannot be separated from the development of the Islamic resurgence movement among young people which emerged in the 1970s. Many ex-activists of the resurgent youth movement have moved into various sectors of life, including into bureaucratic positions.

This chapter focuses on three important themes that have emerged since the late 1980s: 1) the extent of the social, economic and political changes, and the extent to which government is paying more attention to the Muslim community; 2) the Islamic resurgence movement's responses to those changes, particularly changes to their teachings and views about Islam and to the social and political situation; 3) trends among young people in the Islamic movement in 1990s, and their future prospects.

---

[1] A small room or building set aside in a public place for praying.

4.2 Social and political changes

The Islamic revival movement among young people continued to develop into the 1990s, but with a much wider scope and relatively more smoothly. Since the mid-1980s, various Islamic activities, which previously had been conducted informally among Islamic student activists, have been legitimated by the universities. At some universities, such as UNPAD, IKIP and ITB, the mentoring (small Islamic discussion group) progam became compulsory for all Muslim students, and for others studying Islamic religion courses.[2] Such developments were predictable since many Muslim student activists of the 1970s are now becoming lecturers or university staff, and some even have become lecturers on Islamic religion. They are supporters and resource persons for Islamic education on the campuses where they work, and in Islamic proselytizing generally.

In the public sphere, those activists who now hold government and bureaucratic positions continue to spread Islam wherever they work. They initiate and organise Islamic activities in their offices. They hold small gatherings or Islamic discussions, which often develop into bigger events. During the month of Ramadan, Islamic activities are especially pervasive and intense. Breaking the fast together (*buka puasa bersama*), followed by *tarawih* (Ramadan optional night prayer) and sermon has become a routine program during Ramadan. Furthermore, employees try to create an Islamic atmosphere at their office by expressing the Islamic greeting *asslamu 'alaikum*, even at formal events. Women continue to wear veils, a custom which is becoming more widespread.

The 1990s period was also marked by wide-spread and aggressive *dakwah* (Islamic proselytisation) attempts through the mass media. Besides various Islamic magazines, which grew rapidly in popularity from the early 1980s, various Islamic scholarly journals have emerged including *Ulumul Quran, Islamika, Ma'rifah* and *Kalam*. Moreover, on 3 January 1993, ICMI launched a national newspaper *Republika*, to which Muslims responded enthusiastically. In only six months, the circulation of the *Republika* increased from 45,000 to 120,000. Many Muslims, as one informant said, hope that *Republika* can compete with the dominant Catholic and Protestant newspapers, which have for a long time been regarded a presenting distorted news about Islam and Muslims.[3]

Islamic proselytising is now prevalent on almost all television and radio stations. In addition to the printed mass media, the frequency of Islamic programs has increased considerably. Every Thursday night, all television stations, including private stations such as RCTI, SCTV, TPI and ANTV, broadcast religious

---

[2] In some cases, as an informant said, a Muslim can choose to study Christian, Catholic, Hindu, or Buddhist religions. He said that although he is Muslim, he did not choose an Islamic course, but rather chose to study Buddhism (Interview 29 May 1994).

[3] Although, there has been a newspaper, *Pelita*, which is often regarded as a Muslim newspaper, it has not attracted a majority of Muslims because of its poor quality of reporting, and managerial problems.

programs.[4] Moreover, similar programs are presented at about 5 a.m. every morning on all private television stations. These programs include "Di Ambang Fajar", "Hikmah Fajar", "Kuliah Subuh" and "Mutiara Subuh" (all of them have similar meaning ie. morning sermons).[5] The source persons or the speakers in these programs vary from *ulama* and Muslim intellectuals to government bureaucrats, including some government ministers. Also appearing as the speakers are people, such as Imaduddin, who were formerly regarded as militant anti-government preachers. This is another new phenomenon that has emerged since the early 1990s. During Ramadan the frequency of Islamic programs always increases considerably. Programs include Islamic education, sermons before breaking the fast, movies on Islamic themes, Islam in other countries, live shows from Mecca, and Qur'an recitations at the end of the daily program.

This increased intensity of Islamic proselytizing is also evident on various radio stations. Every morning between four and six am almost all radio stations broadcast *dakwah* Islam (Islamic proselytisation). Because there are so many similar *dakwah* programs when switching from one station to another, one can choose different topics or speakers. The types of program broadcast on radio, as on television, vary from sermons, discussions and interviews to live discussion between the radio announcer and the audience. This latter type of program has become one of the most popular among young Muslims, who talk on air about their personal problems, and ask for solutions based on Islamic values. During Ramadan, *dakwah* Islam on the radio becomes even more prevalent, as on television. Special programs are broadcast every day at the end of fasting (*buka puasa*) and *sahur* (the meal before daybreak).

This pervasive and progressive Islamic *dakwah* has gradually resulted in a widespread demand by the Muslim community for a more Islamic way of life. Along with the development of the *dakwah* movement which increased Muslims' understanding of Islam, many parts of the Islamic community began to realise that aspects of their lives were not in accordance with the teachings of Islam. In mid-1989, for example, one research project reported that some manufactured foods contained pork fat. The rumour spread that several products such as soap and tooth paste were *haram* (forbidden) because pork was used in them. This created a social tension, later demonstrated through a widespread boycott of those products among the Muslim community. Those who already possessed those products, threw them away or destroyed them. The 'pork fat issue' subsided after some senior *ulama* and cabinet members were televised nationally eating these products.

---

[4] Hindu, Buddhist, Catholic and Protestant programs are also broadcasted at different times.
[5] Such morning sermons are not presented on the government television station (TVRI, Televisi Republik Indonesia) because its program begins later than those of private television stations.

After a long and heated polemic, the draft Law on Religious Courts (Rancangan Undang-undang Peradilan Agama, RUUPA) was finally accepted on 14 December 1989 by the House of Representatives (DPR). For Westerners like the *Far Eastern Economics Review* reporter Vatikiotis, this was "a surprisingly generous concession to the Muslim community" (1994:137). According to Munawir Sjadzali, "it is the will of history" (*ini kehendak sejarah*) of a country in which 150 million of its 175 million people demanded such a law (Serial Media Dakwah 8.1989). Historically, there were laws on religious courts from 1750 when they were first introduced by Sultan Agung Hanyokrokusumo of the Mataram empire, but gradually the laws were replaced by the Dutch, until 1937 when they disappeared altogether.

Before the new law was accepted, there was strong objection from Christian groups. As reported in the Christian weekly publication, *Hidup* (No. 7), "RUUPA is an attempt to establish Islamic law [in Indonesia]. A state ruled by a religious law is a state religion… And if religious courts are only for Muslim citizens, this implies [that Indonesia] is an Islamic state" (p.28–9). The Islamic magazine *Serial Media Dakwah* (8:1989) reported that, "It is true that RUUPA will establish Islamic law, which means Islamic law will be applied to Muslims who desire it. The scope of the law is limited to civil law, marriage, grants (*hibah*), inheritance (*waris*) and other similar cases. Therefore, it is not true that religious law will control the state". Lukman Harun, a Muhammadiyah leader, said "I was amazed by those Christians who strenuously objected to the RUUPA, which is not related to them and will not inflict any loss at all upon them" (*ibid.*: 12). The Christian resistance to the draft religious law, according to some Muslims and as reported in *Media Dakwah*, was "a continuation of the Dutch plan to demolish the Islamic community in Indonesia".

In October 1990, there were widespread demonstrations against a tabloid magazine *Monitor*, in big cities throughout Java. The issue started when the tabloid, edited by "Christian editor, Arswendo Atmowiloto," ran a poll to find out "the most admired figures" (*tokoh yang dikagumi*). Publication of the poll result showing that the Prophet ranked 11th, just below the editor of the tabloid, angered Muslims. They were outraged to see the Prophet compared with common people (Tempo 27.10.90:28–32). A wave of demonstrations swept almost all big cities throughout Java, especially those with higher education institutions. In Jakarta the *Monitor's* offices were stoned and destroyed by demonstrators, most of whom were students. Demonstrators demanded that Arswendo be put on trial because he humiliated Islam and disturbed inter-religious harmony (*kerukunan antar umat beragama*). In Bandung demonstrations took place continuously in almost all large university campuses. Demonstrations attended by more than four thousand at each site took place at ITB, UNPAD, IAIN (Islamic State University) and IKOPIN (Indonesian Institute of Management and Cooperation). During these demonstrations they hanged and burned an effigy of Arswendo.

Similar demonstrations also occurred in Yogyakarta, Surabaya and Ujungpandang. According to some senior journalists, the Government through Information Minister Harmoko, was forced to ban the tabloid in order to dampen the increasing Muslim outrage. The banning of this tabloid to meet the demands of the community was the first such phenomenon in the press history of Indonesia (Tempo 3.11.90: 26–30). Muslim anger gradually subsided after the banning of the tabloid, and when Arswendo was put on trial.

The banning of the tabloid and the Muslim reaction towards this phenomenon elicited a variety of responses. Arief Budiman, a sociologist at the Satya Wacana Christian University, tried to plead the case of Arswendo and the *Monitor* by saying that "Arswendo was a victim of a social process which needs a 'scapegoat'. Islamic groups, although constituting the majority of the nation, have a marginal political role" (Tempo 10.11.90:43). A moderate response was made by Abdurrahman Wahid. He regretted the attitude of Muslim society which forced the government to ban the tabloid. According to Wahid, the *Monitor* case arose merely due to carelessness. He regretted those who used religious spirit as a justification for anger, hatred and vandalism. Yet another reaction, like that of UNISBA (Bandung Islamic University) students and Rendra, regretted the banning of the tabloid, saying "If wrong has been done, hold a trial. Do not ban the tabloid... Such banning is not appropriate in the democratisation process we are developing". In contrast to these responses, Nurcholis Madjid maintained that the government act was appropriate because "If the government had not acted, society would have tried (*mengadili*) the case. This is more dangerous" (Tempo 3.11.90). According to Madjid and Amin Rais, the *Monitor* case ruined all attempts to develop inter-religious harmony (*kerukunan umat beragama*) (Tempo 27.10.90). Madjid further explains, "I did not see the *Monitor* case as Arswendo's act as an individual. It was a result of a mechanism, namely arrogance, conceit, indifference, and insensitivity of certain groups, and they should be punished as heavily as possible". What Madjid was referring to was in fact the Christian group which owned Kelompok Kompas Gramedia (KKG), one of the biggest printing and publishing companies in Indonesia.[6]

The Muslim outrage can also be seen as a climax or a peak of Muslim disappointment, especially among young Muslims, not only with the *Monitor* but with all publications of Christian publishers. Among young Muslims, especially those involved in various Islamic movements, there was a belief that the aggressive Christian mission had three aims: first, to convert Muslims to

---

[6] At this point I agree with Arief Budiman's statement that the *Monitor* case and Arswendo was only the scapegoat. From Nurcholis Madjid argument and generally Islamic community, it appears that behind the Muslim's outrage against this case, there has been accumulated feelings of frustration and helplessness against the dominant Christian power on publication in particular and other sectors of life in general. Various theories related to the *Monitor* case were reviewed by Jalaluddin Rakhmat in his *Islam Aktual* (Bandung: Mizan, 1994:64–5).

Christianity; second, to diminish Muslim commitment to Islam; finally, to discourage Muslim children and young people from becoming committed to Islam. These aims were believed to be applied through various facilities including newspapers, magazines, hospitals (inherited from the Dutch colonial).[7] Here, all Christian publications were suspected of being agents of Christianisation. The *Monitor* had long been criticised for its pornographic content which was often seen as a source of moral degradation, especially among the young generation. However, those criticisms were seemingly ignored, and the *Monitor* continued to publish pornographic pictures. Because of this the *Monitor* was known as "the hottest tabloid in Jakarta" (Tempo 3.11.90), and probably in Indonesia, because it was distributed not only in Jakarta but also in other cities throughout Indonesia. Regarding the pornographic themes, Arswendo admitted that "I consciously exploited sex and crime in journalism" (*Ibid*). So demonstrations became aimed at Christian targets as well as at Arswendo. As Zainuddin MZ, one of the most famous preachers, said "arrogance and insensitivity made my Muslim brethren, because of their poverty, become a target for the development of other religions. ... This arrogance and insensitivity was shown by Allah in the figure of Arswendo Atmowiloto" (*Ibid*,:28). These various anxieties resulted in widespread tension among the Muslim community, and when the tabloid published the poll result showing the Prophet as ranking 11th, it triggered an explosion of hidden Muslim annoyance.[8]

Another important phenomenon of the early 1990s was the revoking of 1982 decree which forbade female students from wearing veils at school. On 16 February 1991, the Head of School Education and the Indonesian Council of Muslim Clergy (*MUI, Majelis Ulama Indonesia*), as witnessed by the Minister of Education Fuad Hasan and the Minister of Religious Affairs Munawir Sjadzali, signed a new decree which allowed female students to wear veils at school. This ended eleven years of uncertainty, discrimination and even intimidation. Some women had hovered between being students or not; they were students but they were not allowed to attend classes. Although they were not allowed to attend classes they were not expelled from school. Others were expelled from their school, and others were intimidated through the terror and threat of interrogation. Every week they were interrogated by their teachers, like political prisoners (*Panji Masyarakat* 676.1991). Some of them appealed to the court but were unsuccessful. Wearing veils was prohibited not only among school and university students but also among teachers. A female teacher was fired because she wore a veil. The school headmaster said "If the teachers wear veils, I worry

[7] Interview with Muchtar Adam, 23 December 1993.
[8] Fachry Ali seemed not to agree with this statement, because in his view there must have been someone who mobilised and motivated the mass. The poll result, in his view, had nothing to do with the demonstrations, the main factor in these being the existence of a mobiliser and motivator. I agree that there must be a motivator or a mobilizer; however, how can someone mobilise a widespread demonstration without a common and deep interest among the masses?

that students will wear veils as well". In some cases, including a case at ITB, students who wore veils were not allowed to attend practical work or examinations. In 1989, female Muslims who wore veils were slandered as "food poison disseminator" (*penyebar racun makanan*). As a result of this slander (*fitnah*), some female students were attacked (*Panji Masyarakat* 674.1991:15), and in other cases were even stripped and attacked by a crowd (*Panji Masyarakat* 629.1989:62-3). Islamic school students, and Muslim women who wore veils, were harassed and humiliated. These episodes took place in Semarang, Jakarta, Bogor, Serang. However, the impact of this phenomenon spread widely and strongly influenced other places in Indonesia. It created fear among Muslim women, who became scared to go out wearing the veil (*Panji Masyarakat* 628.1989:18-24). This slander against Muslim women, according to some informants including Hasan Basri, the leader of MUI, was another attempt to discredit Islam by those not in favor of the Islamic resurgence in Indonesia. Outside the UNPAD mosque more than a thousand students demonstrated against the slander, their theme being "We do not acquiesce to *jilbab* (veils) being slandered, we do not acquiesce to Islam being slandered". The demonstration was followed by a *Tabligh Akbar* (big sermon), which was supported by various Islamic preaching institutions in Bandung.

The advent of the 1991 decree allowing female students to wear veils at school resulted from consultations amongst *ulama*, the mass media, community representatives, the Indonesian Intellegence Bureau (BAKIN), the State Minister for control of machinery of the state, the Attorney General and the Minister of Education (*Panji Masyarakat* 676.1991:28). The need for a new act became pressing when cases continued to emerge in a situation where there were no clear laws or solutions. Moreover waves of demostrations and protest continued throughout the big cities, not only in Java but also in Sumatra, Sulawesi and Kalimantan. These demonstrations became much more frequent especially between 1989 and 1991. When the French government allowed female students to wear veils at public schools, Bandung Islamic youth and students demonstrated in front of the French Embassy in support of the French government allowing female Muslim students to wear veils at school. One slogan was "In France the veil is allowed, why not in Indonesia?". Finally on 16 February 1991, the 1982 decree was replaced by the 1991 decree allowing the veil to be worn at school.

In late 1991, the Muslim obsession to have a "more Islamic" banking system was realised when a new Islamic-style bank called Bank Muamalat Indonesia (BMI) was established. This new bank was backed fully by President Soeharto. He blessed the new bank and, together with leading businessmen, contributed to the bank's starting capital. This bank works "in a manner similar to a venture capital company. Depositors are regarded as investors and are allocated a return based on how profitably the bank invests their money. In practice customers are likely to receive a return very close to what conventional banks pay on deposits, but with significantly less protection for their funds" (Schwarz 1994:189). The problem with conventional banking, for many Muslims, derives from the practice of charging interest, which in their view is similar to usury, which is forbidden. More than a year before, in mid 1990, NU (*Nahdlatul Ulama*), under Abdurahman Wahid's leadership, set up a joint venture with Bank Summa to develop a network of rural community credit banks. This attempt was praised by Dorodjatun Kuntjorojakti, Dean of the School of Economics at the University of Indonesia, and Munawir Sjadzali, Minister of Religious Affairs, as "a magnificent idea" that "should [have been] done much earlier" (*Ibid*,: 188-9). However, it was appallingly criticised by the some parts of Muslim community, because the bank charged interest (usury), and perhaps because the Bank Summa was owned by a Chinese Christian, William Soeryadjaya. Unfortunately, Bank Summa was closed in late 1992 because of financial mismanagement. Managing financial matters in Islamic ways continued to develop, when the finance minister officially opened an Islamic style of insurance called "Asuransi Takaful Keluarga" (Perwataatmadja 1994:6).

On 25 November 1993, the government-supported gambling and lottery SDSB (*Sumbangan Dana Sosial Berhadiah*) was closed because of a strong demand from the community. Widespread demonstrations had been triggered in late July 1991 by a statement from the minister for social affairs about the continuation of the SDSB lottery in late July 1991. One week after the minister launched the statement, various Islamic youth and student organisations in Bandung demonstrated to demand that the government close the lottery. Subsequently a wave of demonstrations against the government's supported lottery swept through the big cities such as Jakarta, Bogor, Cirebon, Yogyakarta, Semarang, Surabaya, Medan and Ujungpandang. In contrast to the *Monitor* case, demonstrators were not limited only to students and young people but also included members of the wider community. The demonstrations reached a peak in late 1993, occurring almost weekly in large and small cities alike. The last demonstrations were held in front of Istana Negara (the State Palace) and Bina Graha (the president's office). Such demonstrations, according to State Secretary Moerdiono were "actions which already touched state symbols", and if they were not responded to immediately, they might be used (*ditumpangi*) by other interests that would challenge national stability (Tempo 4.12.1993). Finally, after several sessions in the House of Representatives, the social minister announced that the SDSB was discontinued.

Long before the SDSB lottery, there had been similar types of gambling under different names. In 1986, the government introduced PORKAS, which Muslims viewed as a kind of gambling. In response to Muslim criticism, it was later changed into TSSB (*Tanda Sumbangan Sosial Berhadiah*). After further criticism it was given yet another name KSOB (*Kupon Sumbangan Olahraga Berhadiah*) and finally SDSB, but all of them, in the Muslims' view, remained similar, gambling or lottery. Although demonstrations against gambling practices took place in various places, they were not potent enough to force the government to discontinue the gambling. The government only-changed the name, whenever government support of gambling was criticised. From the government point of view, such practices were not gambling. They constituted the only way to gain financial support for national sports. The anti-gambling contingency, however, did not find this to be a convincing reason, stating that there were many better ways to gain such financial support, including taxes, donations and other *halal* sources. Aside from religious concerns, anti-gambling demonstrators demanded that the government recognise the undesireable impact of gambling on society, such as the decrease of purchasing power (*daya beli*) in lower class communities, the withdrawal of local funds (*dana daerah*) and the increase in crime. Moreover, there was also the issue of mismanagement and corruption, in which an ex-government bureaucrat and a retired general were involved (Tempo, 4:12:93).

In addition to these various phenomena, since 1992 there has been a new phenomenon in the history of the New Order (*Orde Baru*), an increase in the number of Muslim figures who have become members of the House of Representatives. On 1 October 1992, about a thousand representatives were inaugurated, of which 424 were from the biggest fraction, GOLKAR (Golongan Karya), and most of them were important Muslim figures. Among them were *ulama*, such as H. Ali Yafie, KH. Yusuf Hasyim and KH. Ilyas Rukhiyat, KH. Azhar Basyir, Hasan Basri, Tuty Alawiyah, and KH. As'ad Umar; intellectuals and educators, such as Nurcholis Madjid, Watik Pratiknya, Ismail Suny, Marwah Daud Ibrahim and Mukti Ali; bureaucrats, such as Azwar Anas, Abdul Gafur and Akbar Tanjung; and youths and enterpreneurs, such as Ferry Mursyidan and Fadhel Muhammad (*Panji Masyarakat* 734:1992).[9] These representatives came from various Islamic groups and organisations, such as NU, Muhammadiyah, and the Neo-Modernists. This phenomenon, according to many observers, was a genuine "greening" (*penghijauan*)[10] process.

This process necessarily meant that the number of Christian intellectuals in both the House of Representatives and in the cabinet decreased. CSIS personalities, such as AMW. Pranarka, Djisman Simanjuntak, Hadisusastro and Yusuf Wanandi were no longer members of parliament. Previously, this group had been an influential power and became a barometer and 'think tank' within the parliament. Similarly in the new 1993 cabinet there were only four members who were not Muslim, while in the previous cabinet more than ten members were non-Muslim. Many influential Christian figures, such as General Benny Murdani, Radius Prawiro, Adrianus Mooy and Johannes B. Sumarlin (the last

---

[9] Moreover, many of these representatives were ex members of HMI (The Islamic Students' Association).
[10] Green is identified as the color of Islam, so greening means Islamisation.

three names were jointly known as RMS,[11] standing for Radius Mooy Sumarlin), were not named to the new 1993 Cabinet.

The above chronology shows that since late 1989, relations between the Islamic community and the government have become much more intimate. This development cannot be separated in general from the Muslim intellectual movements (see Appendix D), and in particular, from the birth and growth of the Indonesian Muslim Intellectual Association (*ICMI, Ikatan Cendikiawan Muslim se-Indonesia*). ICMI, with its founders and supporters who consist of government bureaucrats, intellectuals and businessmen, has been an accelerator factor in this development. Moreover, ICMI was blessed by the government, especially by president Suharto himself. It was another new phenomenon in Indonesian Muslim history in the New Order era. The establishment of ICMI, however, as I will discuss later cannot be separated from the role of young Muslim activists. My intention here is not to include ICMI as part of the youth resurgence Islamic movement, but to see the connection between the two.

4.3 ICMI: A New Hope

University students in Brawijaya University Malang were worried that potential Muslim leaders and intellectuals were scattered, and that there was no one institution which could unite them. They sought the establishment of an institution in which Muslim intellectuals and leaders could develop friendship bonds (*silaturrahmi*) and communicate with each other to effect collective creativity, which in turn could contribute positively to national development (Pelita, 4.12.1990). A group of students of the Technical Faculty, together with the Islamic Activity Unit (*Unit Aktivitas Kerohanian Islam*) at Brawijaya University planned to hold a symposium from 29 September to 1 October 1990. The theme was "Muslim Intellectuals' Contribution Toward the Take-off Era (*Era Tinggal Landas*)" (Tempo 8.12.1990). This group of students consisting of Erik Salman GD,[12] Ali Mudzakir, Muhammad Zaenuri, Awang Surya and

---

[11] 'RMS' has also another connotation which refers to the Republic of South Maluku (RMS, Republik Maluku Selatan), a Christian pro-Dutch separatist movement. Dr Soumokil proclaimed the establishment of the Republic of South Maluku in Ambon in 1950 because the new republic was dominated by Javanese, Muslims and leftists (Ricklefs, 1993:233).

[12] Erik Salman was the leader of the group, and became the head of the committee of the symposium and of the founding group of ICMI. He was born in Yogyakarta on 31 March 1967, and is an activist of the Islamic preaching institution in his campus, besides being a student activist. He is a board member of the Student Senate of the Technical Faculty at Brawijaya University. His parents are well educated, his mother having a PhD and his father being a dentist who works for the State Owned Oil Company of Indonesia (*Pertamina, Perusahaan Pertambangan Minyak dan Gas Bumi Negara*). His father's job required that he often move from one place to another. Erik Salman attended primary and secondary school in Langsa, Aceh, and high school in Jakarta. During his school years his Islamic education had almost been neglected. Eventually, through campus mosque activities, he began to study Islam intensively. He says, "now I tend to be more interested in studying Islam and preaching. Sometimes, this tendency is much stronger than for the other subjects I have studied so far in the faculty" (Pelita 4 December 1990).

Muhammad Iqbal, later met the Rector of Brawijaya University to promote their symposium plan and, although he "hesitated in the face of the expense and political sensitivity", he gave his permission.

With their rector's permission these students -at their own expense- travelled to promote their ideas and to raise funds for the symposium. In their travels they first met with two prominent Muslim intellectuals Dr. M. Imaduddin Abdulrahim and Drs. M. Dawam Rahardjo, who suggested that they also promote an association for Muslim intellectuals. Through Imaduddin's recommendation they met Emil Salim, the Minister of Environment and later the former Minister of Religion, Alamsyah Ratuperwiranegara. This meeting led these students to meet Habibie, the Minister of Science and Technology who was later nominated as a candidate for the chairmanship of Muslim intellectuals association.[13] Based on support from his colleague ministers and Muslim intellectuals Habibie met President Suharto to promote the idea and ask his permission. Without hesitation, as it was reported, the president says "This is good, you can do it" (Hefner 1993:16–19). In a later development, through the figure of Habibie, who has a close connection with President Suharto, the idea to form an association of Muslim intellectuals was realised in late 1990.[14]

Thus, the students' plan to hold a simple symposium snowballed smoothly to become a national event. On 6 December 1990, a symposium on "Developing Indonesian Society in the 21st Century" (*Membangun Masyarakat Indonesia Abad XXI*) was attended by about 512 Indonesian Muslim intellectuals from various disciplines, professions and backgrounds and was opened by President Suharto. Three days later, Vice President Sudharmono closed the symposium.

From this symposium, certain conclusions were drawn. First, social development, basically, is a transformation process towards better conditions. Therefore, social transformation means improving an individual's quality of life. Second, this transformation has structural, cultural and spiritual dimensions. Therefore changes of these dimensions should take place simultaneously and harmoniously.

---

[13] In the meeting between Habibie and students accompanied by Imaduddin, Dawam Raharjo and Syafii Anwar, Imaduddin stated that "Habibie should have stepped forward, because he has an international reputation, strong integrity and is devout" (Berita Buana, 4.12.1990). He is known as a Minister who always fasts on Mondays and Thursdays. The students said, "we are confused because we do not have a leader or idol. We believe that you can be the idol of young Muslims" (Tempo, 8.12.1990). According to *Kompas* (16.12.1990), there were three reasons why Habibie was promoted and later chosen as the leader of ICMI. First, "he was known because of his intellectuality, especially in aeronautical technology, not only in Indonesia but also in America, Europe and Japan". Second, he was a Muslim intellectual, whose integrity was made exemplary for his *umat* (Muslim community) and nation. Finally, "he showed his commitment to promoting Indonesian development in science and technology, so that Indonesia could compete on the international stage."

[14] For more detail information on the establishment of ICMI see Hefner, 1993:1–35. A similar account was also given by Nurcholis in November 1993, when he spoke on the birth of ICMI at an Indonesia Study Group at the Australian National University, and in a discussion with the Indonesian Students Association at the ANU, Canberra. For detailed information about ICMI see *Documentasi Kliping Tentang: ICMI*, published by CSIS, January 1993 and *ICMI Dalam Sorotan Pers*, published by ICMI Jakrta, 1991.

Third, the goal of the transformation itself is to raise the status of humans to *khalifah* (representatives, successors of God) on earth. Fourth, in the next 25 years there would be structural and cultural changes as a result of development and technology. In this process, conflict between old and new values is inevitable. Structural change will be marked by changes in social behaviour which will be experienced as a clash between the old and new patterns. In such a situation a spiritual base, ie. Islam, is needed. Finally, they agreed to form ICMI, as an institution which could optimise their roles in social, economic and political development as an expression of their gratitude to God's blessings (ICMI, 1990:359–62).

Historically, the birth of ICMI was a unique event in Indonesian history. In terms of protocol, it was quite extraordinary because usually a ceremony is opened by either the President or Vice President, and then closed by a Minister. In addition, the founders of this organisation represent various sectors of Muslim power, and include even those usually critical of the government, such as Imaduddin Abdulrahim. Furthermore, the leader of this organisation is a Minister, who heads various State Companies (BUMN, Badan Usaha Milik Negara) and government agencies, and most importantly is known for his closeness to Suharto.

The birth of ICMI was responded to unfavourably not only by non Muslims but also by other Muslim intellectuals. The latter expressed similar concerns to non-Muslims, especially that ICMI would become a political organisation, which would create sectarianism and primordialism within society, and in turn would threaten the national integrity. There was also a concern that ICMI would become another political means of the government. Abdurrahman Wahid, Deliar Noer and Ridwan Saidi were among those who were not supportive of the birth of ICMI. Wahid said, "let me stay outside managing 'Muslim *kaki lima*' (sidewalk traders), so that there is an Islamic group which is nursing them". He also said that "intellectuality cannot be represented by an institution, and cannot be born in an institution." Furthermore, he said "I do not know Habibie... I only pray for the success of the organisation" (Tempo 9.12.1990). Wahid shares the worry that ICMI will trap Indonesia into sectarianism and primordialism. According to Deliar Noer, ICMI is not an independent (*mandiri*) organisation. Like Wahid, he states "I was asked to sign a letter supporting Habibie. I refused because I do not recognise him. I do not know his way of thinking, especially about Islam. He has never been involved in an Islamic organisation". Deliar Noer worried that ICMI would be used by the government, and said "I hope the establishment of this organisation has no connection with the 1992 general election". Ridwan Saidi, like Noer, also worried that ICMI would become the only mass Muslim organisation (*wadah tunggal*). "Intellectuals," he says, "are not mass" They work individually. They struggle on the basis of truth and do not need mass support" (*Ibid*). Non Muslims responded carefully, with a wait and see approach. *Kompas*, a Catholicowned newspaper (3.9.1991), jokingly describing ICMI as "itch me" (*garuklah saya*), reported "An inter-religion positive pluralism principle clearly does not want a religious group to be facilitated by politics for political interest". Like *Kompas, Suara Pembaruan* (a Protestant-owned newspaper) described its concerns in an editorial, saying:

> Thus, the integralistic state ideology (*paham negara integralistik*) is very appropriate for our very complex (*majemuk*) nation, namely a state ideology which will not attach itself with the majority group, but will accommodate all groups and will respect the uniqueness (*keistimewaan*) of all groups either majority or minority. This ideology, characteristic of our Democracy Pancasila does not approve of the tyrany of the minority (*tirani minoritas*) and majority domination (7.12.1990).

The ICMI founders and supporters responded by demonstrating the irrelevance of those concerns and criticisms. Habibie, for example, said "What is wrong with this intellectual organisation? [ICMI] is not the first intellectual organisation in Indonesia". There have been various intellectual organisations long before the establishment of ICMI. Among the Christian community there is PIKI (*Persatuan Intelegensia Kristen Indonesia*, Indonesian Christian Intellectuals Association), and ICKA (*Ikatan Cendikiawan Katolik*, Catholic Intellectual Association). There is also a Hindu intellectual association called FCHI (*Forum Cendikiawan Hindu Indonesia*. Indonesian Hindu Intellectual Forum). In the same vein, Emil Salim, without explaining his reason, said "I do not agree that the birth of ICMI can be regarded as an attempt to develop primordialism". He also argued that ICMI was not a "test case" step to confront the Christian mission. In a meeting attended by some ICMI figures, he said that the accusation of fundamentalism or sectarianism came from Zionist agents. He further said "I do not understand why some people accuse ICMI of being sectarian. They are unaware that the ICMI program is a national program, that what is being produced by ICMI is, of course, not enjoyed only by Muslims" (Pelita 23.5.1992). In various meetings, Habibie stressed that ICMI is "an open organisation, is not exclusive and is non-political" (Pelita 26.4.1991). He also said that ICMI has no political interest (*politis kekuasaan*). Moreover, he said "ICMI was established not to win for Golkar or other political parties in the general election. ICMI was established to solve problems faced by the whole of society, especially the Indonesian Muslim community (*umat*)" (Suara Karya 3.6.1992). ICMI is a cultural organisation which is scientific (*keilmuan*), open (*terbuka*), free and independent, and formally emphasises a cultural approach process and culturalisation (*pembudayaan*) (Antara 26.10.1992).

While Habibie was promoting ICMI, he often, if not always, talked about one important theme, namely the development of the quality of the Indonesian people (*Manusia Indonesia*). In his speech on the foundation of "Nation Servant

Foundation" (Yayasan Abdi Bangsa, YAB),[15] he pointed out that the development of the quality of the Muslim community is crucial because it means developing more than 85% of Indonesian society. Besides, this development is aimed at improving the quality of Indonesia as a whole (Pelita 18.8.1992). On an other occasion, he stated that Indonesian Muslims should not only participate or become followers (*ikut-ikutan*) but should become initiators, motivators and doers of development (Pelita 6.12.1991). He further said that the Islamic community, which comprises the majority of Indonesia, should not accept being directed and determined by others because in democratic life, the majority should be able to lead and direct the minority and not vice versa (Pelita 13.3.1992).

In the first ICMI national meeting (*Silaknas, Silaturrahmi Kerja Nasional*), which was held on its first birthday (5–7 December in Jakarta 1991), the above theme became the main topic of the meeting. The meeting, attended by 545 participants from 32 delegations throughout Indonesia (ICMI 1992:40), focused on attempts to increase the quality of life of the people, through what was called the "economy of the people" (*ekonomi kerakyatan*). In ICMI's view the economy of the people does not have power or access to production factors, especially financial capital and management. This is because it faces economic powers which are oligopolistic and monopolistic.[16] Moreover, during the meeting there emerged an awareness that the Islamic community is a major element of the nation and has significant role and responsibility to help achieve national goals. However, in reality the Islamic community had been alienated from national and state life. Historically, the Snouck Hurgronje policies facilitated Muslim performance of rituals, but suppressed Islamic political awareness (Suara Merdeka 13.12.1991). The results of these policies were deception (*pembodohan*) and pauperization (*pemiskinan*) of Islamic community, which are still experienced. Distorted information about Islam and the Islamic community has been aimed at reducing the role and pioneering (*kepeloporan*) of Islamic community in national development" (ICMI 1992:47), which in turn has made the Islamic community a peripheral majority. The opposition and non-cooperative attitudes of the Islamic community toward the colonial government, which had been internalised and perpetuated among Muslims groups, put the Islamic community "outside the system" (*di luar system*)[17] in the whole process of development. Based on this consciousness, two major themes emerged: first, increasing the Islamic

[15] This foundation was established in Jakarta on 17 August 1992. It was initiated by 45 social figures and leaders, including 10 ministers, wives of ex Vice Presidents, ex Ministers, ulamas, and the ICMI founders. The goals of this foundation are to help and support ICMI by collecting, managing and supporting funds for ICMI programs and activities (Pelita 18 Augugst 1992).
[16] Such topics which were discussed among bureaucrats and Muslims, were quite *taboo*, since they often included references to the children of President Suharto and to collusion between Chinese conglomerates and bureaucrats.
[17] A similar conception can be seen in McVey's "Faith as the Outsider: Islam in Indonesian Poitics", in James P. Picastori, *Islam in the Political Process*.

community's and intellectuals' awareness of their role and responsibilty in structuring national and state life; second, looking for a more appropriate political format, so that the Islamic community and Muslim intellectuals' potential could have a more positive role in the development process" (*Suara Merdeka* 13.12.1991). The idea to increase the role of Muslim in national and state life continues to be an important topic in the following meetings.[18]

The birth of ICMI and its development to 1994 showed various important characteristics. First, Muslim student activists played a crucial role as initiators. The birth of ICMI was the result of a long struggle by various potential Islamic powers. It was a 'convergence point' (*titik temu*) of two streams of Islamic movements: the Muslim student movement, which emerged in the 1970s, and the Muslim intellectuals movement, which emerged in the late 1960s[19] amid lively (*semaraknya*) and on-going *dakwah* attempts.

Second, ICMI to a degree was able to unite Muslim intellectuals from various "Islamic patterns of thought". In the view of Fachry Ali and Bahtiar Effendy, there are four of these: Islamic neo-modernism,[20] Islamic democratic socialism, Islamic universalism and internationalism, and Islamic modernism (Ali and Effendy, 1986). Another categorisation offered by M. Syafi'i Anwar (1994) divides Muslim intellectuals in terms of their political thought into six, namely: formalistic, substantivistic, transformatic, totalistic, idealistic and realistic (chapter IV). Previous attempts to devise such a unity had always failed. Imaduddin, among others had tried to establish such an organisation. Imaduddin recalls "I wanted to establish an organisation like ICMI. But unfortunately, at the very beginning of the process, the police [military authority] put a stop to it" (Tempo 8.12.1990). Similar attempts were made in the mid-1960s, when about 100 Muslim scholars agreed to establish the Muslim Scholars Association (*Persami: Persatuan Sarjana Muslim Indonesia*), but after ten years, this organisation ceased with the death of its founders (Tempo 8.12.1990:36).

---

[18] A year later, 5–7 December 1992, a second meeting (Silaknas II) was held in Jakarta. About 500 participants both from Indonesia and including expatriots (Indonesian Muslim intellectuals resident in foreign countries either as students or as bureaucrats), attended this meeting (Pelita 7.12.1992). Speaking during the opening ceremony, the Minister of Internal Affairs, General Rudini, stated "ICMI should not be suspected of being connected to the extreme right-wing Islamic power". "If such suspicion exists", he further says, "this is because of suspicion toward Islam as a result of the tragedy of the Darul Islam rebellion" (Merdeka 7.12.1992). Similarly, Suharto's advice, presented by Habibie, reminded ICMI not to experience the same tragedy, ie. extremity and rebellion. Meanwhile, Habibie, in another speech, quoting Alamsyah Ratuperwiranegara, said "the establishment of ICMI has erased shame and fear, which have haunted the Islamic community. Today, the Islamic community is proud of its 'Islamity' (*ke-Islaman*) (Suara Karya 7.12.1992).

[19] See Appendix D.

[20] Neo-Modernism, according to Fachry Ali and Bachtiar Effendy, is a pattern of thought which combines modernism and traditionalism. It is different from modernism which opposed traditionalism. Neo-modernism accommodates both modernist and traditionalist ideas.

Third, there was a new wave of Islamic consciousness, not only among what Geertz called *santri*, but also among *abangan* and *priyayi*. There was a process of "Santri-fication" (Schwarz 1994:174), "greening" (Hefner 1993:11), of the *abangan* and the *priyayi* marked by their growing involvement in Islam. Related to this, Harry Chan Silalahi, a CSIS founder, was quoted by Hefner as saying, "What we saw fifteen or twenty years ago, described by Geertz as [*abangan*] and [*priyayi*], almost does not exist anymore. Today it's clear that the great majority of people want to be more Islamic" (Hefner 1993:31).

Fourth, since many devout Muslims occupied various important positions as government bureaucrats or private enterpreneurs, Muslims, especially those who were previously haunted by an inferiority complex, today are proud of being Muslim. At this stage, as Aswab Mahasin (1990) points out, there is a process of "priyayisation of the santri" or "embourgeoisement" of the santri generations (p.138–46). Schwarz reports "[no] longer is Islam seen as the opiate of the uneducated and economically deprived. Professionals and the middle class increasingly are seeing it as a religion which can provide for their spiritual needs in the context of contemporary society" (Schwarz 1994:174).

Fifth, ICMI became an institution in which various contemporary problems faced by Indonesian society in general and Muslims in particular, are discussed. It encourages open discussions of many topics which previously had been regarded as "taboo" politically, as being subversive. Themes like the inadequacies of contemporary economics, and the inequality of roles and responsibilities of the majority became main topics of discussion. Within ICMI, Muslim group consciousness of their being a majority was raised and the need to play a greater role in nation and state lives was emphasised. ICMI founders and members aimed to redevelop the self-esteem and dignity of the Muslim community, after a very long period of being treated as marginal. The statements of Habibie and other ICMI figures which raised the idea of Muslim marginality implied that there was a kind of inferiority syndrome among not only the ordinary Muslim community but also among Muslim intellectuals.

The above development for many young Muslim activists is a good sign for the Muslim future. They believe that their ideas are now also shared by the bureaucrats and intellectuals. Their idea to have a more Islamic Indonesia to a certain degree has come true. There has been a routinisation of ideas previously proposed by various Islamic youth movements. Ideas that were formerly uniquely characteristic of the Islamic youth resurgence movement are now becoming common ideas among Muslims in general.

4.4 Changes: The Recovered Pain

These changes have been viewed differently by various Islamic youth movements. First, there are those who view these changes positively as clear evidence of a rise in the predominance of Islam. Many formerly critical issues, such as the marginal role of Muslims in Indonesian political, social, economic and cultural life, are no longer concerns. When many Muslim intellectuals and leaders became members of the House of Representatives and became Ministers, their numbers lessened Christian influence in the parliament and in the Cabinet. Some young Muslim activists believe that Islam in Indonesia is no longer peripheral, no longer kept in a 'corner' (*terpojok*) position. The friendly attitude of the government toward Islam is regarded as reflecting purely good intentions for which the Islamic community should be grateful.

Second, other young Muslim activists have responded carefully to the government's action and to recent Islamic developments in Indonesia. They view these as something for which they should be grateful but, at the same time, something they should be wary of. In their view, it is true that there have been some changes in the government's attitude toward Islam, but they question the motives behind those changes. They are worried that this apparent attitude represents a government strategy to gain wider support from the Muslim community. They are worried about being used by others, as previously in Indonesian Islamic history. Despite their worries, they believe that such changes and developments will benefit their movement. They hope that the decline in military suspicion of Islam will create a much wider opportunity for *dakwah* activity. Islamic youth activities, which previously were always suspected as being political activities, today are conducted freely, without the fear of being accused of subversiveness. Nowadays Islamic *dakwah* activities involve almost all strata of society, from the lower to elite classes, from children to older people.

The third view is quite extreme. Some young Muslim activists maintain that as long as an Islamic system has not been adopted across the board and as long as an Indonesian Islamic state has not been established, there has been no significant progress or development. For them, the increasing number of Muslims in the House of Representatives and in the new Cabinet are not signs of advances for Islam in Indonesia. They argue that recent developments are similar to others in the previous history of Islam in Indonesia. Many times, they believe, Muslims have been tricked into unwaranted rejoicing.

It is difficult to pin-point exactly which view belongs to which movement since among those youth movements each of these views is shared among them. Among members of the Young DI movement and ex-LP3K, for example, I found two different views, one which views the social and political changes carefully and moderately and the other which claims those changes have nothing to do with Islamic prospects. In the latter view, "there have been no changes at all as long as the existing regime remains in control." As long as the existing system is not replaced by Islam, there is no significant change.

Similar division can also be seen among other movements. It is quite different in those movements which originated outside Indonesia. Indonesian social and political changes have no significant impact on them, because they already have certain standards which have been drawn up internationally. One informant, a sympathiser (or probably a member) of *Hizb al-Tahrir*, said "it is true that there are some changes within society, but they are nothing as long as the Islamic Caliphate (*Khilafah Islam*) has not been established (in Indonesia or internationally) and as long as Muslims' thought is far from the true Islamic thought." This is an example of the extreme view.

Unlike the Young DI, LP3K and *Hizb al-Tahrir*, the *Darul Arqam* and *Jamaah Tabligh* seem to be happy (or not bothered) with those social and political changes. This is perhaps because they put more emphasis on ritual aspects and are less concerned with social and political matters. *Jamaah Tabligh* for example always tries to avoid even talking about political matters. *Darul Arqam*'s view toward those changes can be found in a book written by its leader Ashaari Muhammad, *Presiden Suharto Ikut Jadual Allah* (President Suharto Follows God's Schedule). In this book he supported President Suharto for doing the pilgrimage to Mecca, and praised him for becoming a much better Muslim. On the evidence of this view, these movements belong to the first category which view these changes positively as clear evidence of a rise in the influence of Islam.

Despite these differences of opinion, political, social and cultural changes have inevitably influenced Islamic resurgence movements among young people. During the development period, those revivalist movements encountered resistance and criticism from many parts of the community and the government. Moreover, with various changes within society, they in turn were forced to change certain aspects of their movement to suit current social and political situations. Therefore, in order to survive and to make their ideas more acceptable to a wider community, they modified their original doctrines, their methods of education, their syllabus, and their views of the current social and political situations. During this adaptation process they were often trapped into internal conflicts, which often ended in disunity (*perpecahan*) among them. Although all of the movements tried to adapt to the current situation, their degree of adaptation varied considerably.

The adaptation process resulted in new trends among the resurgent Islamic youth movements. Previously, most of them were quite radical, and they paid more attention to increasing Islamic emotional attachment. Since the late 1980s Islamic youth movements have varied in how radical they are. At least two major trends developed among young Muslim activists: namely 'activism' and 'intellectualism.' The former trend is seen among young Muslim activists who put more emphasis on Islamic activism and behaviour, that is concrete and visible application of Islam. They believe that Islam should be applied comprehensively to daily life activities, including those of the individual or of the community. Today, in their view, Islam is not visible in Muslims' daily activities, and consequently the blessing of God and His glory have never been gained by Muslims. The intellectualism is represented by those who believe that the thinking (*pemikiran*) of the Islamic community should be enlightened, and that Muslims' understanding of Islam should be reconstructed. They argue that the main cause of various problems faced by Muslims is due to intellectual weakness and backwardness. Unlike other activists, they pay more attention to the intellectual aspects of Islam.

The activist camp is divided into five categories: ritualists, mystics, radicals, philanthropists and fun-seekers (*hura-hura*). Ritualists are those young Muslim activists who stress the 'ritual' aspect of Islam, or the concrete aspects of Islam. They wish to practise Islamic activities, exemplified, they believe, by the Prophet (*sunnah*), and they call these practices "rituals". According to them, the Islamic community has strayed from the *sunnah*. Such a tendency can be seen clearly, for example, among the *Darul Arqam* and *Jama'ah Tabligh* movements. They wear a special type of clothing, wear beards and moustaches, have special ways of eating and other behaviour, which they believe are *sunnah*.

The mystics emphasise the mystical aspects of Islam. They seem to be unsatisfied with those Islamic organisations and movements that are devoid of the mystical aspects of Islam. They began to involve themselves in various *tariqat* (Islamic mysticism) orders. In the Bandung pesantren *Bengkel Ahlak Darut Tauhid* (see Appendix E), about four thousand people, mostly students each week, attend sermons which always finish with a kind of "collective confession" during which all attending cry. An informant said that through this kind of sermon "I experienced the pleasure of crying". As in *tariqat* orders *santri* are also introduced to a package of *dzikir* (recitation).

The third category are the radicals including those who wish to change, revolutionarily and immediately, the existing system including the government into an Islamic system. According to this group, the world is divided into two sides: the Islamic (God's system) and the non-Islamic (*thaguth* or *jahiliyah*).[21] These two sides, in their view, cannot accommodate one another. Furthermore, they view every aspect of life from this radical 'black or white' perspective. Since the present system is non-Islamic, it should be changed as soon as possible. Within this category, there are usually *imam* (leaders), who take their followers' oaths (*membaiah*). Included in this category of radicals are the Young Darul Islam movements, and Islamic youth movements which are genealogically related to the Darul Islam movement.

---

[21] *Thaguth* means evil or anything worshipped that is other than God. *Jahiliyah* (state of ignorance) refers to pre-Islamic paganism and pre-Islamic times.

The philanthropists stress the social aspects of Islam. In their view, Islam should help and assist people who are poor, who have suffered and who are oppressed. For them, freeing peple from their suffering means applying Islam to other people. Such a tendency derives from their dissatisfaction with other Islamic organisations which neglect the social aspects of Islam. Their activities are directed toward helping people in rural areas, or in the slums of urban areas. Their activities include teaching children who do not go to school, helping at orphanages, being readers for the blind and other social actions.

'Fun-seekers' represent a new trend among young Muslim activists. They are more interested in fun activities but their actions are still inspired by Islamic teachings. This tendency, I believe, is a response to other Islamic groups and activities, which they view as too strict and rigid to accommodate those of an elite and Westernised younger generation. This young elite Westernised group has found psychological and social difficulties in involving themselves in many existing Islamic activities. Besides ordinary religious sermons, they often hold glamorous activities, such as big artistic performances, concerts, dances and other big events. One channel of development for this category is through various radio stations. In Bandung, one of the favourite stations is the Ardan radio station, and in Jakarta Prambors Rasisonia radio station (Tempo 29:4:1994).

The intellectuals can be divided into three sub-categories: philosophers, pseudo-scientists and Islamic-experts (*tafaquh fial-din*). The first includes those who focus on Islamic philosophy in particular and philosophy in general. They try to revitalise Islamic philosophy through various study centers and Islamic higher education. The pseudo-scientists are Muslim activists who try to seek scientific explanations of Islamic teachings. They argue that Islam, and the Qur'an in particular, are scientific, and the true Islam, for them, should be scientific Islam (*Islam yang ilmiah*). The last category of Islamic experts is more interested in Islamic knowledge in general and Islamic law in particular. This tendency can be seen clearly in the emergence of various *Pesantren Mahasiswa* (University student pesantren), which like ordinary *pesantren*, teach their santris (students) Islamic knowledge. In Bandung, there are at least two *Pesantren Mahasiswa*, namely *Miftahul Khair* (Key of Goodness) and *Fi Zhilal al Quran (In the Shade of the Qur'an)*.[22] Similar types of pesantren have also been established in other cities such as Bogor and Yogyakarta.

Compared to activism, intellectualism tendency seems to have a much better future. First of all -unless there are dramatic political changes- a more stable social and political climate will give a greater possibility to the development of this trend, and at the same time militate against the development of activism, especially the radical one. Activism can easily develop in a situation where

---

[22] This name is taken from the book of Sayyid Qutb *Fi Zhilal al-Qur'an*, 30 volumes of Qutb's comment on the Qur'an.

ideological conflicts frequently occur, or in a time of political turmoil. Second, the next period of Islam, as Kuntowijoyo (1985:71–7) points out, will be a period of "ideas and science" in which the Islamic community, including young people, become more enlightened. This is a period when modern communication technology will give Muslims a wider access to information, including information about the Islamic *ummat* in other parts of the world and about the diverse views of Islam.

 The emergence of these idiosyncratic categories of Islamic youth movements shows that in conjunction with the social, political and cultural changes in Indonesia, Islamic resurgence movements among young people also change. In response to resistance and criticism from the community, they modify their original teachings and doctrines by adding, emphasising, playing down and eliminating certain aspects of their own movement. Because each movement has responded differently, there is greater variation in the emphases of the movements. Some of these categories already existed before, but they developed and spread more widely in the 1990s, when they gained more followers than before. The influence and popularity of some other categories declined.

This stage, borrowing Weber's term (1947:358–373), is the routinisation of charisma, a phase in which charismatic ideals and practices are transformed -either traditionalised or rationalised, or a combination of both- into a "permanent routine structure." In Weber's view this transformation is based on "(1) the ideal and also the material interests of the followers in the continuation and the continual reactivation of the community; (2) the still stronger ideal and also stronger material interest of the charismatic leader in continuing their relationship." Similar to Weber, Anthony F. C. Wallace (1979:427) named this stage as the routinisation stage in which effective actions and programs of the movement in "nonritual spheres [reduced] stress-generating situations, ... [and] established as normal economic, social, and political institutions and customs."

Chapter 5: Conclusion: Continuation of *TAJDID* Tradition

> At the turn of each century there will arise in this *ummah* those who will call for a religious renewal (the Prophet Muhammad, in Abu Daud, Cairo 1348)

The argument developed in this thesis is that contemporary Islamic resurgence among young people in Bandung, Indonesia, is a continuation of *tajdid* (renewal) tradition in Muslim societies. Current Islamic resurgence is another form of Muslim internal transformation that attempts to maintain the Muslim commitment to the fundamental principles of Islam and to reconstruct an Islamic society in accord with the Qur'an and the *Sunnah* (Traditions of the Prophet). The *tajdid* movement has always been related to two aspects of Muslims' lives -the spiritual and the worldly-which cannot be separated. The former refers to an attempt to purge Islamic teachings and practices of non-Islamic influences and to present it once again in its original pure forms. The latter refers to an endeavour to solve social, economic, political, and cultural problems faced by the Muslim community.

Like previous reformist movements such as the Muhammadiyah movement (founded in 1912) and Persatuan Islam movement (founded in 1923), current Islamic resurgence attempts to call Muslims to return to the basic teaching of Islam, the Qur'an and *sunnah*. The difference is that the contemporary Islamic movement not only promotes purification of Islamic beliefs and rituals from *bid'ah* (innovation), *khurafat* (superstitions) and pre-Islamic traditions and practices but also promotes purification of much wider aspects of Muslims' lives, including economic, social and cultural institutions and practices, from both foreign and native non-Islamic influences.

Similarly, like Muhammadiyah and PERSIS which -directly or not- struggled for Indonesian independence from the Dutch colonial domination, current Islamic movements, also have the same spirit, ie. to free themselves from another form of domination. This refers to the idea that the overwhelming Muslim majority (during the New Order) has always been marginal and under the domination of certain minority groups. It also refers to foreign cultural domination which is believed to threaten Muslim identity.

Like previous Islamic reform movements, the contemporary Islamic movement arose both from within the local tradition of Islam and undoubtedly under the influence of international Islamic movements. Previously, the international influence was limited in terms of ideas and merely spread through personal communication or books which only arrived in Indonesia after long delays.

There was thus a clear time gap between the Islamic movement in Indonesia and other parts of the world. This is very different from the contemporary Islamic movement. Through the advance of electronic mass media international influence is not limited to the slow spread of Islamic ideas. Islamic ideas can spread rapidly and widely regardless of national boundaries. Moreover, this globalisation era enables one movement in one Muslim country not only to spread its ideas but also to establish its branches in other countries. The growth of the global system reinforces the notion of the unity of the Muslim community (*ummah*).

This study examines current Islamic resurgence in three stages of development. The first stage which I called the foundation of the movement, refers to the early emergence of the movement in which certain individuals experienced spiritual dissatisfaction. Through these individuals the idea of dissatisfaction spread widely in particular social, political, economic and cultural conditions. The next stage was the development of the movement in which these individual figures and their followers established various organisations through which the Islamic resurgence ideas spread in agressive and pervasive ways. The conditions of the early emergence remained similar. Both stages were characterised by emotional and radical features. The third stage was routinisation of the movement, a phase in which social, political, economic and cultural conditions were transformed into more desired conditions. In response to this transformation various Islamic groups changed their original teachings and doctrines to adapt to the new conditions. These new conditions also created a new ground for the emergence of new types of Islamic movements ie. mystic and intellectualistic.

This study confirms the "processual structure" of revitalisation movements of Anthony F.C. Wallace. Islamic resurgence in Bandung, however, seem to be in conflict with his prediction that "Human affairs around the world seems more and more commonly to be decided without reference to supernatural powers." (1979:428). He further argued that:

> ... the evolutionary future of religion is extinction. Belief in supernatural beings and in supernatural forces that affected nature without obeying nature's law will erode and become only an interesting historical memory. To be sure, [religious movement] is not likely to occur in the next generation; the process will very likely take several hundred years, and there will always remain individuals or even occasional small cult groups who respond to hallucination, trance and obsession with a supernaturalist interpretation. But as a cultural trait, belief in supernatural powers is doomed to die out, all over the world, as a result of the increasing adequacy and diffusion of scientific knowledge ... the process is inevitable (1966:264–5).

In contrast with Wallace prediction, the forgoing survey shows how modern people in a globalisation era become much more attached to religion not viceversa.

Furthermore, the study of Islamic resurgence among young people in Bandung shows that, as Nakamura says, "Islam [in Indonesia] has been getting stronger" (1983:181). This also confirms Victor Tanja's statement that "the history of Islam in Indonesia is a history of expansion (*perluasan*) of santri civilisation and its influence on religious lives, social and politics in Indonesia. ... Despite the presence of various obstructive factors, the foundation for santri influence, which is gradually broadening, has been built." This broadening influence of santri, in the 1980s, is marked by the process of "santrinisation" or "santrification" of the *priyayi* (Schwarz 1994), also known as *Islamisasi Birokrasi* (Islamisation of bureaucracy). At the same time there are also process of "embourgeoisement of santri" (Mahasin 1990) or the "priyayisation of santri" and the "intellectualisation of santri" (Anwar 1994:212). These processes created what many observers have called a "santri middle class" which has filled various positions from bureaucrats, entrepreneur, academics to NGO activists. At this point, Geertz's dichotomisation of santri and priyayi seems to have been diffused, if indeed it exist (*Ibid*,:214, cf. Harry Chan Silalahi in Hefner 1993:31).

This tendency seems to continue to develop along with the growth of the santri middle class, the renaissance of Muslim intellectuals and the more accommodative attitude of the government toward Islam. This tendency is also associated with a new orientation of Islam in Indonesia, that is, cultural Islam not political or ideological Islam. The future trend of young Muslim activists, along with this general tendency, seems to be more intellectual in its nature but at the same time strictly attached to the fundamental sources of Islam.

The tendency of the Islamic resurgence movement among young people toward a more intellectual nature cannot be separated from the ideas proposed by the Muslim intellectuals movement. The intellectuals endeavour to shift Islamic values as scientific conceptions which balance out various established conceptions, including social and economic conceptions (Anwar 1994:225). This seems to be in conjunction with the concerns of the youth movement of Islamic resurgence which wants to apply Islamic values in all aspects of the Muslims' lives. One of the most important evidence of this was the birth of ICMI in 1990 in which the paths of two movements, of Muslim intellectuals and Muslim youth, converged at the same point.

Islamic resurgence is a global phenomenon throughout the Muslim world; however, it is unique from one culture to another. Unlike Islamic resurgence in the Middle East, Islamic resurgence in Indonesia did not take its form in radical political activism and revolutionary action. There was a tendency toward political and revolutionary activism, but it carried little power. The common tendency rather is more cultural in nature, ie. "an attempt which does not challenge dramatically and in revolutionary terms the established social and cultural system through political and military force. [It is Muslims'] attempt to colour and fill the established social and cultural building with Islamic spiritual and moral perspectives" (Anwar 1994:226). This Islamic cultural strategy, as Munawir Sjadzali said, "creates a comfort atmosphere, invites sympathy and creates a much better relation between Islamic community and the New Order government (*Mizan* 1990:49–53)."

Appendix A: The Meeting Forum of Islamic Campus Preaching Organisations

The second meeting was held in Salman ITB at January 1987. The meeting was titled *Sarasehan Antar Lembaga Dakwah di Kampus*. During the meeting the word *Sarasehan* was changed to *Silaturrahim*, an Arabic word meaning brotherhood or friendship bond. According to an informant who was involved in the meeting, use of the word *Saresehan* was criticised because it came from Javanese, seen as the source of *Kejawen*.[1] This second meeting resulted in several agreements. They agreed to hold coordinated activities involving active participation by Islamic Preaching Institutions on many campuses. These coordinated activities were Islamic Training (*Dauroh Dirosah Islamiyah*) in IPB Bogor, Preaching Management Training (*Latihan Management Dakwah*) in Salman of ITB, Muslim Women's Training (*Bina Wanita dan Keluarga*) in all LDK and publication of the bulletin *Al-Urwah*.[2] Another agreement was that Salman of ITB should become the Coordinating Centre for Campus Islamic Preaching Institutions for all of Java (*Pusat Komunikasi Lembaga Dakwah Kampus se-Jawa*).

The third meeting was held in September 1987, at Air Langga University. Delegations from 30 important universities in Java attended this meeting. Two important agreements arose from this meeting. First, the name of meeting was changed to *Forum Silaturahim Lembaga Dakwah Kampus (FSLDK*, Forum of Campus Preaching Institutions), by which it is still known. Second, the forum agreed on a set of basic required activities (*kegiatan standar internal*) for a campus preaching institution. The delegations also agreed to keep the forum informal, without either a leader or an organisational structure. The intention was to keep the forum independent and free from pressures that could threaten the *dakwah* movement. There was concern that if the forum had a formal organisational structure like other Islamic organisations it would be easily infiltrated and coopted by other interests.[3]

In the following meeting (1988) of the "Forum of Campus Islamic Preaching Institutions in All Java" (Forum Silaturrahim Lembaga Dakwah Kampus (FS-LDK) se-Jawa), another important step was taken. Participants agreed to formulate a set of guide lines for Islamic Preaching Institutions in Campuses comprising

---

[1] *Kejawen* is mysticism associated with the Javanese view of the world, and general Javanese knowledge. Javanese beliefs and traditions were regarded by many participants (most of them Javanese) as un-Islamic.
[2] An Arabic word meaning 'link'. It was taken from The Qur'an, chapter 2: 256. This name is similar to the political journal of Jamal al-Din al-Afghani *al-Urwat al-Wuthqa* (The Most Solid Link).
[3] These could be government authorities, especially army intellegence operatives, and other groups which were believed always to be hostile to Islam. Included here were Christian elites.

directions, aims and targets of *dakwah* attempts to revive Islam as shown by the Prophet. Through these guidelines, activists hoped to create a common perception of direction for the *dakwah* movement. These guidelines were called *Khittah* LDK. *Khittah LDK* could not explain all aspects of *dakwah* or provide a comprehensive understanding of it. *Khittah* LDK was only a brief and practical guide which often did not suit the different campus conditions. To fill in the gaps, the forum agreed to develop *Mafahim* (understanding), a set of LDK conceptions (*cara pandang* LDK) regarding three fundamental issues in Islam, namely *aqidah* (basic faith), *shariah* (Islamic law) and *dakwah*. The *Mafahim* was prepared by a committee consisting of a few representatives in consultation with some *ulamas*. After it was reviewed by a special meeting in Pesantren Ngruki, in central Java, the *Mafahim* was later distributed to all Campus Islamic Preaching Institutions in Java, and on some campuses *Mafahim* became the source reference for Islamic education (*pembinaan ke-Islaman*).

Since 1989, when the fifth meeting was held in IKIP (Teaching and Education Institute) Malang, the scope of the forum has been widened to include all of Indonesia. The name itself was changed to *Forum Silaturahim Lembaga Dakwah Kampus se-Indonesia* (Forum of Campus Preaching Institutions in All Indonesia). Participants at the meeting not only came from Islamic Preaching Institutions on Javanese university campuses but also from other islands in Indonesia. Attending the meeting were delegations from Sumatera, Sulawesi, Nusa Tenggara and Bali. This was an attempt to the spread the *dakwah* movement to other campuses in big cities outside Java. Moreover, the idea was also put forward by some activists of Islamic Preaching Institutions outside Java who had attended the meeting as observers (*peninjau*). By 1994 the forum had been convened nine times. Every year the scope of the meeting became much wider and the number of participants increased.

In the Bandung and the East Priangan region, FSLDK is held every year hosted in turn by various universities. In early 1994, the FSLDK meeting was hold for the ninth time, this time in Mandala College of Technology (*Sekolah Tinggi Teknologi Mandala*) Bandung. About 60 delegates from Islamic preaching institutions from various colleges, academies and universities attended this meeting. They came from most parts of West Java, including Sukabumi, Cianjur, Karawang, Bandung, Sumedang, Cirebon, Tasikmalaya and Ciamis (DKM Baiturrahman STTM, 1994). Some of the universities had already established Islamic preaching institutions on their campuses, such as ITB and UNPAD, but others were still planing to do so even if they did not have any idea what an Islamic preaching institution is. The meeting identified one of its aims as being to encourage campuses with established institutions to share experiences with others that do not have one, encouraging and helping them.

Appendix B: The Nature of Reformist and Modernist Islam

These terms, 'reformist' and 'modernist,' refer to Islamic groups or individuals who believe that the Islamic community drew on stagnating ideas (*kejumudan pemikiran*) and was trapped in diverge act mysticism, superstision (*khurafat*), innovation (*bid'ah*), and even worse, that Islamic community had fallen to Western (Christian Europe) domination. To solve these problems, they asked and persuaded Muslims to reanalyse and reinterpret Islamic doctrines in a language and formulation that would be accepted as 'modern thought'. Islam should be understood rationally and should be presented in a form that was appropriate to the contemporary situation, so that Islam would be able to compete with the modern civilisation. Through this way, it was believed, the Islamic community (*umat Islam*) would be able to free themselves from Western colonialism, poverty, ignorance and backwardness, and would return to the real situation of Islam, in which Islam was superior to other powers.

Reformist attempts center on three issues. First is purification of Islamic doctrines and practices (*fiqh*, jurisprudence, law covering all aspects of life including rituals) from superstition (*khurafat*), innovation (*bid'ah*), and un-Islamic influences and traditions, which are commonly accepted by Muslims as proper Islam. The second issue concerns the Islamic political movement, ie. independence movements against the Dutch colonial domination and suppression. The third issue is Islamic educational and social movements which are marked by the adoption of Western (Dutch) organisational and educational systems and ideas, including those of Christian missionaries, without violating Islamic principles. The result of this adoption was the establishment of Islamic schools, social and political organisations, scout movements and missionaries with modern Western (Dutch) methods and techniques. Among these three issues, the first issue, i.e. the *fiqh* issue became the most important issue, often creating tension among Muslim groups. Because of this, modernists and reformists often concentrate only on the *fiqh* issue.

These reformist and modernist ideas were represented by Islamic organisations such as Muhammadiyah, Persatuan Islam (PERSIS, Islamic Unity), Al-Irsyad, Jamiatul Khaer and Sarikat Dagang Islam (SDI, Muslim Trade association) which later became Sarekat Islam (SI, Muslim Association). The roots of these movements can be traced back to the Islamic purification movement of Muhammad ibn Abd al-Wahab, the Pan-Islamic political struggle of Jamal al-Din al-Afghani, the Muhammad Abduh reformist movement and other movements developed in the Middle East, especially in Mecca and Cairo. These reformist and modernist movements, since they challenged Islamic traditionalists, later provoked the establishment of the *Nahdlatul Ulama* (NU, the Rise of Religious Scholars), which was worried that Islamic traditions would dissapear (Ali and Effendy 1986).

Sociologically, there are two distinct characteristics of the reformist and modernist movements. First, different from traditionalist groups which centered in rural areas (*pedesaan*) and developed among peasant community, they commonly developed among educated and entrepreneur circles in urban areas (*perkotaan*). This tendency, according to Fachry Ali and Bahtiar Effendy, derives from two different responses of religious figures (*ulama*) toward the Western (Dutch Christian) cultures. The traditionalist circles tended to avoid Western penetration and isolated themselves from contact with Western agents by establishing religious institutions, educational and other social institutions exclusively in rural areas. This isolation strategy, Ali further argues, was even more strengthened and justified by the Prophet Muhammad's words *"man tasyabbaha bi qoumin fahuwa min hum"*: Those who imitate (traditions of) a group of people are part of them. On the contrary, modernist circles, usually businessmen and educated people in urban areas, had closer contact with the Western culture and its agents which clearly existed in urban areas.

The second sociological characteristic of the reformist and modernist movement is that the followers and supporters are usually of the younger generations. The radical reformist approaches and rebellious attitudes toward traditions and practices existing in the Islamic community, attracted young people. Borrowing Ben Anderson explanation in his *Java in time of Revolution: Occupation and Resistance 1944–1946*, young people played more of a role than the elite intellectuals in the Indonesian revolution. This important role of young people in Java, Anderson argues, is based on the Javanese cultural view that youth is the period of isolation, transition and independence, which is potentialy rebellious (Anderson, 1972:2–7, cf. Hadiz's, 1992:22–3 and Tholkhah, 1994:8–9). Young people, who came from of the traditionalist circles in rural areas, were acquainted with the modernists ideas in urban areas, where they studied or worked. When they returned to their country areas they spread what they learned in cities. As a result of this, there was an inevitably conflict between the young modernist generation and older traditionalist generation (Noer, 1973:6, 216–46).

Appendix C: International Islamic Movements and Their Presence in Indonesia

Ikhwan al-Muslimin was established in 1928 in Ismailyya, Egypt by Hasan al-Banna, a charismatic figure who later became the first leader of the movement. He was born in Mahmudiyya, a small town in the Nile delta, in 1906 in a strong Muslim middle class family. His father was a sheikh and the Imam of a mosque, who was also a student at the Al-Azhar in the time of Muhammad Abduh, one of the most important figures of Islamic modernist tradition in Egypt. After finishing his study at the local Teacher Training College, Hasan al-Banna continued his study at Dar al-Ulum College in Cairo. In his school days, Banna involved himself in various Islamic associations which emphasised individual religious and moral reform and on commitment to preach Islam to other Muslims by visiting mosques, public entertainment centres, coffee houses and other public gatherings. When he graduated in 1927, he joined the government service and served as a teacher in a Ismailiyya primary school but finally resigned in 1946.

Hasan al-Banna's experience in Cairo greatly influenced his idea to establish the Muslim Brethren (*Ikhwan al-Muslimin*) movement. In Cairo he met Rashid Rida (1865–1935) and his *Salafiyya* (Islamic reform) movement which promoted political and social aspects of Islamic reform, the need for an Islamic State and the introduction of Islamic law. Hasan al-Banna was also attracted by Rida's ideas of total Islamic self-sufficiency and of the danger of Westernisation. At the same time, in Cairo he also saw the presence of British political and cultural domination which threatened traditional Egyptian society and Islam. The Westernisation threat, he believed, came not only from British colonial officials, but also from Westernised Egyptian elites who attempted to replicate Western models of political, social and economic development.

Hasan al-Banna, like Rashid Rida, saw Western secularism and materialism as the major causes of Egypt's political, social and economic problems, and of Muslim impotence and decline. Hasan al-Banna believed that only through return to Islam, following the Qur'an and the example (*sunnah*) of the Prophet, would Muslim all over the world recover from their ilness. Different from his modernist predecessors, who were deeply concerned with Western learning, he stressed the perfection and comprehensiveness of Islam and its self-sufficiency. Concerned with these problems, he then formed Islamic discussion groups. Later in 1928, a year after he finished his study at the Dar al-Ulum College he established the movement called *Ikhwan al-Muslimin*, the Muslim Brethren. Hasan al-Banna who was the "unique embodiment of the Sufi spiritualist, Islamic scholar, activist leader who possessed a rare ability to evoke mass support by translating doctrinal complexities into social action" (Dekmejian 1985:80) made the movement develop rapidly.

There is no clear information about when exactly this Islamic movement came to Indonesia. However, from various books written by many members of *Ikhwan al-Muslimin*, which were later translated into Indonesian, it appears that the ideas of the movement reached Indonesia in the early 1970s. From the translation books which were used by various Islamic youth groups in Indonesia in their early development, it is clear that among other movements, *Ikhwan al-Muslimin* played the most important role. It is also not clear whether this movement has a formal branch in Indonesia or not. However, there are many young Muslim activists who regard themselves as member of *Ikhwan al-Muslimin*. Among Islamic youth activists, it is often called 'IM'.

Hizb al-Tahrir (Liberation Party) was established in 1953 in Lebanon by Taqiyuddin al-Nabhani, a great thinker, politician and Jerussalem Supreme Judge. The movement spread throughout the Middle East especially in Jordan. The main aim of this movement, as stated in its constitution, was to carry out Islamic life and to re-establish a *Khilafah Islam* (Islamic Caliphate). Ideas of the movement were introduced to Indonesia from 1987, mostly in some large cities of Java, such as Jakarta, Bogor, Bandung, Yogyakarta and Surabaya, and especially on university campuses. Books and papers about this movement had limited circulation among university students.

As admitted by one of its propagandists, *Hizb al-Tahrir* as an exclusive movement does not exist in Indonesia. However, its ideas have been spread systematically through a method of education called *halaqah*, a study group under an *Ulama*. Within the *halaqah*, about 23 reference books are studied, including *Nizham al-Islam* (the Islamic way of life), *al-Nizham al-Iqtisadi fi al-Islam* (the Islamic Economic System), *Al-Shakhsiyat al-Islamiyah* (Islamic Personality), and *Naqd al-Isytiraiyat al-Marksiyah* (Critique of Socialism-Marxism). Like other movements, this one tried to apply Islam to all aspects of daily life. However, practical and symbolic matters, such as ritual practices and moral attitudes towards television, and music, were left up to members themselves.

In Indonesia, as in other countries where this movement developed, the movement spread its ideas secretly. In Iraq, Syria, Lybia, Jordan, Egypt and Tunis many figures of this movement were arrested and killed. For this reason, *Hizb al-Tahrir* became an underground movement. Some of the reference books were even buried by members of the movement for security reasons. Because of the need for secrecy, relations amongst branches of the movement in various countries were very weak. This is turn led to large differences in the *Hizb al-Tahrir* movement from country to country.

Another movement was *Darul Arqam* (Arabic Dar al-Arqam, Arqam territory).[1] Members of this movement can be identified easily by their clothes and features. Male members usually wear a long dark or grey dress, and a turban. They also usually have a thin moustache and a beard. Female members usually wear black clothes which covered all parts of their body, except their eyes. They open their veils (*cadar*), which cover their faces, when they are in a female area or when they are among their *muhrim* (unmarriageable relatives)[2] Another distinct characteristic of members is their practice of eating together from the same container. In Indonesia, especially in Bandung, this movement has developed and attracted students since early 1990.

This movement was established in Malaysia in 1972 by Muhammad Suhaimi. Suhaimi was born in Wonosobo, Central Java in 1295 Hijri (1917). According to members of Arqam, Suhaimi was the 33rd descendant of the Prophet Muhammad. In Singapore and Malaysia Suhaimi created controversy, when he taught a *wirid* (recitation), called *Awrad Muhammadiyah*. According to his followers, this *wirid* was directly given by the Prophet inside the Ka'bah in Mecca. The *wirid* consists of reciting 50 times the *istighfar* (*astagfirullah*, I ask God's forgiveness), reciting the *al-Ikhlas* chapter of the Qur'an, and reciting 50 times the *Shalawat Nabi* (invocation of the Prophet). This *Awrad Muhammadiyah*, which is believed to diverge from true Islamic teachings, became one of the reasons that Darul Arqam was banned in Indonesia in 1994. Already, in 1990, the West Sumatran MUI (Assembly of Indonesian Ulama) had banned this movement for the same reason. Darul Arqam was also banned in Malaysia in 1994 because of its ultimate aim to apply the Prophet's preaching strategy, i.e. to create an Islamic village that would develop into a wider region and finally into an Islamic state. Malaysian government accused the Darul Arqam of preaparing arm forces, which threatened national security (Panji Masyarakat 21:7:1994).[3]

---

[1] Arqam was the name of one of the Prophet's companions. In the early period of Islam, his house became a secret centre for the spreading of Islam; a meeting place of the Prophet and His followers, and a place to educate new coverts.

[2] In Arabic *mahram* means 'forbidden'. In Islamic law, it is the degree of consanguinity between a man and woman that renders marriage impossible but gives them the right of association.

[3] On 20 October 1994, Ashari Muhammad, ex-leader of the Darul Arqam which has been banned since 5 August 1994, admitted in front of Malaysian *ulama* and *mufti* (official expounder of Islamic law) that the Darul Arqam teachings, especially *Awrad Muhammadiyah*, were wrong and conflicted with Islamic teachings. He also admitted that he made stories about his meeting with the Prophet in order to assure his followers. Furthermore, he promised to correct and reeducate his followers who had been lost. In this meeting Ashaari Muhammad, who always wore a long dark cloth and turban, wore a white Malay cloth and a white cap (*peci*) without turban. Likewise, his wife, who usually wore a black veil that covered her face, wore the usual veil that only covers hair, neck and shoulder (Panji Masyarakat 1:11:1994). His confession raised then question whether he honestly and consciously admitted his wrong doing or did so merely because he was forced to do so to save himself, his followers and his movement from the government restrictions. How he could easily and suddenly change his mind after 26 years was difficult to understand. Would he be able to change his followers' beliefs and practices?.

Jama'ah Tabligh is another Islamic movement that has attracted many young people, most of them students. Like Darul Arqam, female followers usually wear dark clothes which cover all parts of their body. Male members usually have a moustache and beard. Their practice of eating from the same container using their hands and sitting on the floor are similar to the habit of Darul Arqam members. The differences is that they wear special Indian-style clothes, and they always use a *siwak* (tooth brush made of speical wood). They claim that all of these habits identified them as the *sunnah* (tradition) of the Prophet.

This movement was established in India in 1930 by Syaikh Malik Maulana Muhammad Ilyas (1887–1948). According to its members, the emergence of this movement was inspired by the fact that the Muslim mentality had degenerated, and that mosques were empty. There was no other solution except to resume the teachings of the Prophet. One of its main activities is called *khuruj* (to go out), which means to go out to do *dakwah* (preaching). Members usually walk from house to house, from mosque to mosque, and this is not limited by country boundaries. Senior members of the movement usually visit various neighbouring countries.[4] During *khuruj*, members usually stay at the mosques they are targetting. According to this movement, *khuruj* activity can be done for about three days a week, a month in a year, or at least 40 days in a whole lifetime.

Their *khuruj* activities usually start with visiting Muslim families and inviting them to come the mosque to pray. One member of the *khuruj* group, which usually consisted of less then ten persons, gives a *bayan* (speech) after prayer. The speeches, according to the constitution of the movement, would deal with politics or *khilafiyah* (differences in the Muslim community in matters of doctrinal importance); would not ask for charity or talk about others' mistakes; and would not humiliate the government, other groups or particular individuals. The movement's slogan, according to a member of *Jama'ah Tabligh*, was "if there is something wrong correct it immediately, and do not engage in polemic" (Tempo 3:4:1993).

From these Islamic groups emerges an important issue. Although they have similar ideological views and orientation ie. to solve problems faced by the Muslim *ummat*, they differently identify what these problems are. These differences have resulted in offering different solutions and emphasising different aspects. This is especially the case among those Islamic groups which come from overseas, such as the Middle East and India, since they originally emerged in different countries with different causes, different historical backgrounds and different cultural settings. These imported Islamic groups although they do not

---

[4] One of my students, at the IAIN, told me that he had visited Thailand, Singapore and Malaysia, although he had been a member for only two years.

neglect local Indonesian situations, arere concerned with international Islamic issues.

Appendix D: Muslim Intellectuals' Movement at Glance

Since Indonesian independence, in 1945, along with the process of educational democratisation, there has been a strong demand for education, including tertiary education (Ranuwiharjo 1991:53). Because of their underprivileged condition, in terms of status and finance, very few students, who came from santri background, had access to higher education (Tempo 14.6.1986). In the 1960s, when the number of higher level education institutions increased rapidly, students from santri circles began to have a wider access to continue their study to the tertairy level. The result of this was that in the 1970s those students who graduated from various tertiary educational institutions began to occupy bureaucratic positions in the government, and some of them became involved in private and business circles.

In the political sphere, however, they did not give voice to their view, especially because at that period, as McVey (1983:199) puts it, the New Order regime of Suharto "[restricted much more] the political and social role of Islam than the preceding leftist government of Sukarno had dared". Such restrictions, as a matter of fact, had been experienced by Indonesian Muslims since the late 19th century, when the Dutch began to colonise the Indonesian archipelago. The Dutch realised that Islamic political power threatened their domination. C. Snouck Hurgronje, the architect of Dutch policy on Muslims affairs, discouraged any Islamic involvement in politics (McVey 1983:200). Later, long after the Dutch and other colonial powers left the Indonesian archipelago, the Islamic de-politisation process continued to take place.

From such a continuous restriction, Muslims became much more aware of the sensitivity of an Islamic attribute in political sphere, since it had always been identified as anti-government and with rebellions to establish an Islamic state. Moreover, they also became aware of the continuous political defeat experienced by Muslims by other powers on the political stage. This awareness led to the need for a new "format" (Ma'arif 1993:177) or "break through" (Tempo June 1986) of Islam in its involvement in Indonesian development in general. In the late 1960s, Indonesian Muslim intellectuals set out a new step of Islamic history in Indonesia. Instead of expressing Islam through political jargon, they promoted what was called "cultural Islam". By this new strategy, they tried not to be involved in mass politics, instead they applied a cultural approach to Islamic revitalisation, which in the long term would neutralise military and government suspicion and strengthen the "roots of Islam in the nation as a whole". According to this new view, Islam should not serve as a political ideology, but as a "source of ethical and cultural guidance" (Hefner 1994:4, cf. Ali 1986:175–191).

The emergence of this Muslim intellectual movement cannot be separated from the role of Nurcholis Madjid, an ex-leader of the Islamic Students' Organisation (HMI, Himpunan Mahasiswa Islam). One of the most controversial themes proposed by him was "Islam, yes. Islamic Party no". In his view, "there is nothing sacred, except Allah. Islamic parties are not sacred, therefore, it was wrong to say that those who did not vote for the Islamic party were not Muslim" (Tempo June 1986). In 1970s, this idea was criticised as being "secular", that is trying to separate Islam from political life. Various strong criticisms came from Islamic militant groups, including various Islamic movements which began to develop in the same period of time. Despite these criticisms, this Islamic cultural approach with its friendly (*ramah*) image gradually gained support from Muslim intellectuals, and the most important point was that the government seemed not to be allergic to this new format of Islam. Relations between Muslim intellectuals and the government became much more intimate, in the sense that those who promoted cultural Islam either voluntarily or forceably supported government policies. This could be seen for example when the government launched a "Mass Organisation" act, which forced all Islamic organisations to replace their foundation (*azas*) with Pancasila. Almost all Muslim intellectuals, after a heated polemic, supported or accepted the rule. In the view of militant Muslims, such a decision was a major defeat for Muslims. Such accomodative attitudes of Muslim intellectuals towards the government might be understood also as the only way to survive in an emergency situation (*darurat*), because if they openly opposed or disagreed with government policies, they took risks. For more detail information about Muslim intellectual movement, its history, classification, and its role in national development see Federspiel's *Muslim Intellectuals and National Development in Indonesia* (New York: Nova Science Publishers, 1992). See also Muhammad Kamal Hasan, *Muslim Intellectual Responses to "New Order" Modernization in Indonesia* (Kuala Lumpur: Dewan Bahasa dan Pustaka, 1980), Fachry Ali and Bachtiar Effendy, *Merambah Jalan Baru Islam* (Bandung: Mizan, 1986), and M.Syafi'i Anwar's thesis, *Hubungan Islam dan Birokrasi Orde Baru: Study tentang Pemikiran dan Perilaku Politik Cendikiawan Muslim dalam Orde Baru 1966–1993* (Jakarta: Fakultas Pasca-Sarjana Universitas Indonesia, 1994).

Appendix E: Moral Workshop Daarut Tauhid: a New Trend among the Youth

Daarut Tauhid was established in September 1990 in Bandung by Haji Abdullah Gymnastiar, a young *ustadz* (religious teacher) who always wears a white shirt, a sarong and a white turban. It is not really an Islamic movement, in terms of distribution networks and ideological views, but it is similar to an ordinary pesantren in Indonesia. However, in term of its influence on young Muslim activists in Bandung it is quite significant. In December 1993, about four thousand people were attending weekly sermon at the pesantren, most of whom were university students and school students, who came from various places throughout West Java.

The main activity of this pesantren, like other pesantren, is daily study of Islamic subjects, especially *Tawhid* (Unity of God) and *Dzikir* (recitation). *Dzikir* here does not refer to any classic book of *dzikir*, like *Al-Adzkar* of Imam Nawawi (one of the great Indonesian *ulama*, whose books became a text book in many pesantren throughout Indonesia). Abdullah Gymnastiar tries to develop a type of *dzikir* based on a book written by Hasan al-Banna, a leader of *Ikhwan al-Muslimin*. Once a week there is always a public sermon which is attended by approximately four thousand people. At the end of this weekly sermon, Agim, as he is affectionately known, usually asks the audience to reflect on their previous deeds, and gradually the audience becomes more self-reflective. Finally, the thousand-strong audience breaks down and cries (Risnawati 1993).

The full name of Abdullah Gimnastiar's pesantren is *Bengkel Akhlak* (Moral Workshop) *Daarut Tauhid*. With this pesantren, Abdullah Gymnastiar wanted to create Muslims who were "intellectual, devout, and entrepreneurial" (*ahli pikir, ahli dzikir, and ahli ikhtiar*) (*Tempo* 3.4.1993). Furthermore, he wanted to develop a new strategy and pattern of *dakwah* in order to make *dakwah* more effective (Risnawati 1993). This pesantren organises not only ritual activities, but also economic and social activities. By 1994, it had 14 businesses including printing, public transportation, retailing and computer rental. Its assets were more than Rp. 175 million and each month it earns about Rp. 40 million. From its name, *Bengkel Akhlak* it can be understood that this pesantren has become a place to rehabilitate the morality of its students. According to Gymnastiar, youngsters who come to the pesantren, generally become better citizens (*Tempo* 3.4.1993).

Glossary

Aqidah (Arabic)	A statement of doctrine, or an article of faith.
Bai'ah (Arabic)	'Contract' or oath of allegiance binding members of an Islamic sect or Sufi *tariqa* to their spiritual guide.
Bid'ah (Arabic)	Innovation; a view, thing or mode of action that has formerly not existed or been practised. The term has come to suggest change in religious belief or action that leads to heresy, but not necessarily to disbelief.
Dakwah (Indonesian from Arabic da'wa)	Missionary or propagatory activities, to call or invite mankind to believe in the true religion, Islam. This word also means to make Muslims better Muslims.
Darul Islam (Arabic Dar al-Islam)	Realm of Islam; those lands under Muslim rule.
Fiqh (Arabic)	Understanding of *syari'ah;* the system of jurisprudence based on the *usul fiqh* (roots or foundation of jurisprudence).
Harakah (Arabic)	Originally means 'movement.' In Indonesia it refers to various independent Islamic movements which are not formally approved by government.
Haram (Arabic)	A sanctuary which is forbidden by the *shari'a* (Islamic law).
Imam (Arabic)	One who stands in front to lead the *shalat* (prayer), and who leads the Muslim community.
Jihad (Arabic)	War against unbelievers in accordance with shari'a. Also applied to an individual's struggle against baser impulses.
Jama'ah (Arabic)	Group or community.
Jilbab (Arabic)	Long, loose robe worn by Muslim women activists over regular clothes. It also often refers to *kerudung*, a head-dress that reveals only the face. It falls down loosely to below the chest or the waist.
Khutbah (Arabic)	The sermon delivered on Fridays at the noon prayer. The khutbah is also given in the morning after sunrise at the 'Idul Fitri (end of Ramadan) and 'Idul Adha (Sacrifice festival).

Mihrab (Arabic)	Niche or chamber in the front part of mosque where the *imam* (leader) leads prayers and *khatib* (preacher) gives the sermon.
Mubaligh (Arabic)	Originally means bearer or messenger; A Muslim propagandist or preacher.
Muhammadiyah (the Way of Muhammad)	One of the most significant Islamic modernist organisation of Indonesia, established in 1912.
Mujahid (Arabic, pl. Mujahidin)	Soldier fighting a holy war or *Jihad*.
Mujaddid (Arabic)	The person who leads *tajdid* (renewal).
Musholla (Arabic)	A small room or building set aside in a public place for praying.
Pengajian (Indonesian)	Learning the Qur'anic recitation; religious lecture; public sermon.
PERSIS (Persatuan Islam)	An Islamic modernist organisation -established in 1923-played important role in the debate between traditionalist and modernist viewpoints in religious matters.
Pesantren (Javanese, Pondok Sundanese)	Islamic school with fully boarding students.
Pesantren Kilat (Indonesian)	Short course of Islamic training activity. It also refers to an Islamic group or movement.
Priyayi (Javanese)	Aristocrate, court official.
Ramadan (Arabic)	The holy month in which the Qur'an was revealed. It is the fasting month in which Muslims may not eat, drink or have sexual intercourse during the daylight hours.
Sahur (Indonesian from Arabic sahira meaing to stay up at night)	Having meal before dawn during fasting.
Santri (Sundanese)	Student in *pesantren*. It also refers to a pious Muslim.

Shalat (Arabic)	Ritual worship performed five times daily, one of 'five pillars' (*rukn*) of Islam.
Syari'ah (Arabic)	Sacred law of Islam which governs all aspects of a Muslim's life. It is elaborated through the discipline of *fiqh*.
Subuh (Indonesian from Arabic subh)	Dawn; daybreak.
Sunnah (Arabic)	Custom sanctioned by tradition of the Prophet enshrined in *hadits*.
Tajdid (Arabic)	Renewal, regeneration of the commitment to the fundamental principles of Islam and the related reconstruction of society in accord with the Qur'an and the sunna.
Thagut (Arabic)	An idol, tempter to error, something worshiped other than God. Among Muslim activists in Indonesia this refers those who hostile to Islam, especially intellegence operatives. *Tahajud* (Arabic) Optional prayer after midnight.
Tarawih (Arabic)	Optional prayer at night during the month of Ramadan.
Tawhid (Arabic)	Unity of God. It is a fundamental tenet of Islam.
Ulama (Arabic singl. 'alim)	Those Muslims who are considered knowledgeable in religious learning, particularly in jurisprudence and theological matters.
Ummat (Indonesian from Arabic ummah)	Community of believers, in particular the community of Muslims.
Usrah (Arabic)	Family; One type of Islamic education among young Muslim activists, in which small and solid groups of activists discussed Islam and developed a sense of brotherhood. It was first introduced by *Ikhwan al-Muslimin* (Muslim Brethren) in Egypt.
Ustadz (Arabic)	Religious teacher.
Zakat (Arabic)	Religious duty imposed on all Muslims to give a portion of their wealth, as prescribed by religious law, in alms to the poor. It is one of the 'five pillars' of Islam.

Bibliography

Books

Abdulrahim, M. Imaduddin. *Kuliah Tauhid.* Bandung : Pustaka Salman ITB, 1980.

Abdulrahim, M. Imaduddin, "Memahami Kebangkitan Islam di Malaysia" in Anwar, Zainah, *Kebangkitan Islam di Malaysia*, Hasannain (trans.). Jakarta : LP3ES, 1990.

Abdulrahim, M. Imaduddin, *Apakah Ugama Islam Itu?* Kuala Lumpur : Persatuan Mahasiswa Islam Institut Teknoloji Kebangsaan, Malysia.

Aberle, David F., "A Note on Relative Deprivation Theory as Applied to Millenarian and Other Cult Movements," in Thrupp, Sylvia L. (ed.) *Millenial Dreams in Action Essays in Comparative Studies.* The Hague : Mouton & Co., 1962.

Ahmad, Khurshid, "The Nature of Islamic Resurgence," in Esposito, John l. (ed.), *Voices of Resurgent Islam,* New York : Oxford University Press, 1983.

Alam, Jafar, *Ikhwan ul-Muslemeen,* Dacca : Islamic Foundation Bangladesh, 1980.

Al-Faruqi, Ismail R., "Islam and Zionism," in Esposito, John L., *Voices of Resurgence Islam,* New York : Oxford University Press, 1983.

Ali, Abdullah Yusuf, *The Meaning of The Holy Qur'an,* Maryland : Amana Corporation, 1991.

Ali, Fachri and Saimima, Iqbal A.. 'Merosotnya Aliran Dalam Partai Persatuan Pembangunan', in *Analisa Kekuatan Politik di Indonesia: Pilihan Artikel Prisma.* Jakarta : LP3ES, 1985.

Ali, Fachri, and Effendy, Bachtiar, *Merambah Jalan Baru Islam: Rekonstruksi Pemikiran Islam Indonesia Masa Orde Baru,* Bandung : Mizan, 1986.

Ali, Fachri, *Mahasiswa, Sistem Politik di Indonesia dan Negara,* Jakarta : Inti Sarana Aksara, 1985.

Ali-Fauzi, Ihsan and Bagir, Haidar (eds.), *Mencari Islam,* Bandung : Mizan, 1990.

Anderson, B.O., *Java in a Time of Revolution Occupation and Resistance, 1944–1946,* Ithaca : Cornell University Press, 1972.

Anwar, Syafi'i, *Hubungan Islam dan Birokrasi Orde Baru Studi tentang Pemikiran dan Perilaku Politik Cendikiawan Muslim dalam Orde Baru –*, thesis in Political Science at Post Graduate Faculty, University of Indonesia, Jakarta, 1994.

Anwar, Zainah. *Islamic Revivalism in Malaysia: Dakwah Among the Students.* Kuala Lumpur : Pelanduk Publication, 1987.

Anwar, Zainah, *Kebangkitan Islam di Malaysia, Pengantar: Imaduddin Abdulrahim.* Hasannain (trans.). Jakarta : LP3ES, 1990.

Any, Anjar. *Dari Cicendo ke Meja Hijau: Imran Imam Jamaah.* Solo : CV. Mayasari, 1982.

Arsalan, Al-Amier Sjakib, *Mengapa Kaum Muslimin Mundur dan Mengapa Kaum Selain Mereka Madju,* Chalil, Moenawar (trans.), Jakarta : Bulan Bintang, 1967.

Ayoob, Mohammed (ed.), *The Politics of Islamic Reassertion,* London : Croom Helm, 1981.

Ayubi, Nazih N., *Political Islam: Religion and Politics in the Arab World,* London : Routledge, 1991.

Aziz, Drs, Abdul, Drs. Imam, Tholkhah, Drs., Soetarman (eds.). *Gerakan Islam Kontemporer di Indonesia.* Jakarta : Pustaka Firdaus, 1989.

Banna, Al-Imam Hasan, *Usrah dan Dakwah,* Kuala Lumpur : Ikhwan Agensi, 1979.

Benda, Harry J., *Bulan Sabit dan Matahari Terbit: Islam Indonesia pada Masa Pendudukan Jepang.* Jakarta : Pustaka Jaya, 1980.

Boland, B.J. *Pergumulan Islam di Indonesia.* Jakarta : Grafiti Pers, 1985.

Cantory, Louis J., 'The Islamic Revival as Conservatism and as Progress in Contemporary Egypt," in Sahliyeh, Emile (ed.), *Religious Resurgence and Politics in the Contemporary World,* New York : State University of New York Press, 1990.

Crosby, Faye, J., *Relative Deprivation and Working Women,* Oxford : Oxford University Press, 1982.

CSIS. *Dokumentasi Kliping tentang NKK Reaksi dan Tanggapan.* Jakarta : CSIS, 1980.

CSIS, *Dokumentasi Kliping tentang Asas Tunggal.* Jakarta : CSIS, 1985.

CSIS, *Dokumentasi Kliping tentang ICMI,* Jakarta : CSIS, 1993.

Curran, Daniel J. and Renzetti, Claire M., *Social Problems* (second edition), Massachusetts : Allyn and Bacon, 1990.

Dekmejian, R. Hrair, *Islam in Revolution: Fundamentalism in the Arab World,* New York : Syracuse University Press, 1985.

Denny, J.A. *Gerakan Mahasiswa dan Politik Kaum Muda Era 80-an.* Jakarta : Miswar, 1990.

Dessouki, A.E. Hillal. *Islamic Resurgence in The Arab World.* Newyork : Praeger, 1982.

Djamari, H. et. al. *Laporan Penelitian Kegiatan Kemakmuran Mesjid di Kotamadya Bandung (Studi Kasus),* Bandung : Institut Keguruan dan Ilmu Pendidikan Bandung, 1988.

Emerson, Donald K. "Islam in Modern Indonesia Political Impasse, Cultural Opportunity," in Stoddard, Phillip H. et al, (eds.), *Change and the Muslim World,* New York : Syracuse University Press, 1981.

Engineer, A. Ali. *Islam in South-East Asia.* Delhi : Ajanta Publications, 1985.

Esposito, John L., ed. *Voices of Resurgent Islam,* New York : Oxford University Press, 1983.

Esposito, John L., *Islam and Politics,* New York : Oxford University Press, 1984.

Esposito, John L., *Islam in Asia: Religion, Politics and Society,* New York : Oxford University Press, 1987.

Esposito, John L., *Islamic Threat Myth or Reality?,* Oxford : Oxford University Press, 1992.

Etzioni, Amitai and Etzioni, Eva, *Social Change: Sources, Patterns and Consequences,* New York : Basic Books inc. Publishers, 1964.

Farhang, Rajaee, "Islam and Modernity: The Reconstruction of an Alternative Shi'ite Islamic World View in Iran," in Martin Marty, E. and Scott Appleby, R. (eds.), *Fundamentalism and Society: Reclaiming the Sciences, the Family and Education.* Chicago : The University of Chicago Press, 1993.

Federspiel, Howard M., *Muslim Intellectual and National Development in Indonesia,* New York : Nova Science Publishers Inc. 1992.

Federspiel, Howard M., *Persatuan Islam Islamic Reform in Twentieth Century Indonesia,* New York : Modern Indonesia Project Southeast Asia Program, 1970.

Feith, Herbert, "Pemikiran Politik Indonesia –: Suatu Pengantar", in Budiardjo, Miriam, *Partisipasi dan Partai Politik,* Jakarta : Gramedia, 1982.

Feuer, Lewis S., *The Conflict of Generations: The Character and Significance of Student Movement,* New York : Basic Books, 1969.

Geertz, Clifford, *The Religion of Java,* Chicago : The University of Chicago Press, 1960.

Gellner, Ernest, *Muslim Society,* Cambridge : Cambridge University Press, 1981.

Gellner, Ernest, (ed). 1985. *Islamic Dilemmas: Reformers, Nationalists and Industrialisation.* Berlin : Mouton Publishers.

Gerth, Hans H., "The Nazi Party: Its Leadership and Composition", in Mclaughin, Barry, *Studies in Social Movements: A Social Psychological Perspective*, New York : The Free Ptress, 1969.

Gungwu, Wang, "The Study of the Southeast Asian Past," in Reid, Anthony and Marr, David (eds.), *Perceptions of the Past in Southeast Asia*, Kuala Lumpur : Heinemann Educational Books (Asia) LTD, 1979.

Haddad, Yvonne Y. et. al. *The Contemporary Islamic Revival A Critical Survey and Bibiliography*, New York : Greenwood Press, 1991.

Hamka, Rusydi and Are Saimima, Iqbal Emsyarip (eds.), *Kebangkitan Islam dalam Pembahasan*, Jakarta : Yayasan Nurul Islam.

Hasan, Muhammad Kamal, *Muslim Intellectual Responses to "New Order" Modernisation in Indonesia*, Kuala Lumpur : Dewan Bahasa dan Pustaka Kementrian Pelajaran Malaysia, 1980.

Hasan, Riaz. *Islam Dari Konservatime sampai Fundamentalisme.* Jakarta : Rajawali, 1985.

Haq, Obaid, "Islamic Resurgence: The Challenge of Change" In Abdullah, Taufik and Siddique, Sharon (eds.), *Islam and Society in Southeast Asia.* Singapore : Institute of Souteast Asian Studies, 1986, 332–48.

HMI, *Keputusan Kongres HMI ke-X.* Jakarta : Pengurus Besar HMI: 1972.

Husaini, Ishak Musa, *Muslim Brethren (Al-Muslimin)*, Lahore : The Book House.

ICMI, *Silaturrahmi Kerja Nasional (Silaknas) I Ikatan Cendikiawan Muslim Se-Indonesia: Laporan Penyelenggaraan Jakarta, 5–7 December 1991*, Jakarta : ICMI 1992.

ICMI, *Membangun Masyarakat Indonesia Abad XXI, Prosiding Simposium Nasional Cendikiawan Muslim 1990*, Jakarta : ICMI, 1991.

ICMI, *ICMI Dalam Sorotan Pers Desember 1990-April 1991*, Jakarta : ICMI, 1991.

ICMI, *Silaturrahmi Kerja Nasional (SILAKNAS) III Ikatan Cendikiwan Muslim se-Indonesia (ICMI), Laporan Penyelenggaraan Jakarta 4–6 Desember 1993*, Jakarta : ICMI, 1994.

The Islamic (Student) Association of Cairo University, "Lesson From Iran" in Donohue, John J. and Esposito, John L. (eds.), *Islam in Transition: Muslim Perspectives*, New York : Oxford University Press 1982.

Jenkins, David. *Suharto and His Generals: Indonesian Military Politics 1975–1983.* Ithaca : Cornell Indonesian Project 1984.

Jainuri, A., *Muhammadiyah: Gerakan Reformasi Islam di Jawa pada Awal Abad ke-Duapuluh*, Surabaya : Bina Ilmu 1981.

Kartini, Tintin, Dampak Aktivitas Lembaga Dakwah Kampus (LDK) Terhadap Pengamalan Keagamaan Mahasiswa (Study Comparatif antara LDK IAIN, UNPAD, ITB dan IKIP Bandung), Final paper at Communication Faculty, IAIN Sunan Gunung Djati Bandung, 1992.

Khoury, Philip S., "Islamic Revivalism and the Crisis of the Secular State in the Arab World: A Historical Appraisal" in Ibrahim, I. (ed.), *Arab Resources: The Transformation of a Society*, London : Croom Helm 1983.

Kumar, Krishan, (ed.), *Revolution: The Theory and Practice of a European Idea*, London : Weidenfield and Nicolson 1971.

Lipset, T.M. and Altbach, P.G. (eds.), *Students in Revolt*, Boston : Houghton Miffin & Co, 1969.

Maarif, A. Syafii. *Studi tentang Percaturan dalam Konstituante: Islam dan Masalah Kenegaraan.* Jakarta : LP3ES, 1985.

Maarif, A. Syafii, *Peta Bumi Intellektualisme Islam di Indonesia*, Bamdung : Mizan 1993.

Madjid, Nurcholis. *Islam Kemodernan dan Keindonesian.* Bandung : Mizan 1987.

Mahasin, Aswab, "The Santri Middle Class: An Insider's View" in Tunter, Richard and Young, Kenneth, *The Politics of Middle Class Indonesia*, Clayton (Victoria Australia) : Center of South East Asian Studies, 1990.

Marty, Martin E. and Scott Aplleby, R. (eds.), *Fundamentalisms Observed*, Chicago : The University of Chicago Press 1994.

Marty, Martin E., *Fundamentalism and Society: Reclaiming the Sciences, the Family and Education.* Chicago : The University of Chicago Press 1993.

Masjid UNPAD. *Materi Mentoring Al-Islam Universitas Padjadjaran.* Bandung : Madjid UNPAD Bandung 1993.

Maududi, S. Abul A'la, *A Short History of the Revivalist Movement in Islam*, Lahore (Pakistan) : Islamic Publications LTD., 1981.

McLuhan, Marshall M. and Quenten, Fiore, *War and Peace in The Global Village*, New York : Bantam Books 1968.

McVey, Ruth, "Faith as the Outsider: Islam in Indonesian Politics", in Piscatory, James P. *Islam in The Political Process.* New York : Cambridge University Press 1983.

Munson, Henry, *Islam and Revolution in the Middle East*, New Haven : Yale University 1988.

Muzaffar, Chandra, *Islamic Resurgence in Malaysia*, Petaling Jaya : Penerbit Fajar Bakti Sdn Bhd 1987.

Muzaffar, Chandra, "Islam in Malaysia: Resurgence and Response," in Asghar, Ali Engineer, *Islam in South-East Asia*, Delhi : Ajanta Publications (India), 1985.

Muzaffar, Chandra, "Islamic Resurgence: A Global View," in Abdullah, Taufik and Siddiqui, Sharon (eds.), *Islam and Society in South East Asia*, Pasir Panjang (Singapore) : Institute of Southeast Asian Studies, 1986.

Muzani, Saiful (ed). 1993. *Pembangunan dan kebangkitan Islam di Asia tenggara.* Jakarta : Pustaka LP3ES.

Naipaul, V.S. *Among the Believers: An Islamic Journey.* London : Andre Deutsch 1981.

Nakamura, Mitsuo, *The Crescent Arises over The Banyan Tree*, Yogyakarta : Gadjah Mada University Press 1980.

Natsir, Tatan M., *Di Sekitar Reformasi dan Modernisasi Masyarakat Islam.* Bandung : Al-Ma'arif, 1972

Noer, Deliar. *Indonesia and Islam.* Jakarta : The Risalah Foundation 1991.

Noer, Deliar, *Partai Islam di Pentas Nasional 1945–1965*, Jakarta : Grafiti Press 1987.

Noer, Deliar, *The Modernist Muslim Movement in Indonesia 1900–1942*, Singapore : Oxford University Press 1973.

Othman, Mohd Dahari, Communication and Charisma: A Case Study of Religious, Political and Social Forces in Malay Village. PhD thesis at the Iowa State University, 1990.

Perry, John A. and Perry, Erna K., *The Social Web: An Introduction to Sociology*, New York : Harper & Row, Publishers, 1988.

PERSIS, *Qanun Asasi/Qanun Dakhili PERSIS*, Bandung , 1991.

PERSIS, *Tafsir Qanun Asasi Persatuan Islam*, Bandung : Pusat Pimpinan Persatuan Islam 1967.

Poerbakawatja, Soegarda, *Pendidikan Dalam Alam Indonesia Merdeka*, Jakarta : Gunung Mulia 1970.

Qutb, Sayyid, *Milestones [Ma'alim fi al-tariq]*, Kuwait : New Era Publishers 1978.

Qutb, Muhammad, *Islam The Misunderstood Religion*, Lahore (Pakistan) : Islamic Publications LTD., 1980.

Rahardjo, M. Dawam, "Gerakan Mahasiswa: Sebuah Refleksi," in Denny, J.A. *Gerakan Mahasiswa dan Politik Kaum Muda Era 80-an*, Jakarta : Miswar 1990.

Raillon, Francois. *Politik dan Ideologi Mahasiswa Indonesia: Pembentukan dan Konsolidasi Orde Baru 1966–1974*. Jakarta : LP3ES, 1985.

Rakhmat, Jalaluddin. *Islam Aktual*. Bandung : Mizan 1994.

Ramazani, R.K., *Revolutionary Iran Challenge and Response in The Middle East*, Baltimore : The Johns Hopkins University Press.

Ranuwihardjo, Sukadji, "Equity, Quality and Efficiency in INdonesia's Higher Education System," in Hill, Hal (ed.), *Indonesia Assessment 1991*, Canberra : Department of Political and Social Change RSPaS, ANU, 1991.

Reid, Anthony and Marr, David (eds.), *Perception of The Past in South East Asia*, Kuala Lumpur : Heinemann Educational Books (Asia) LTD, 1979.

Ricklefs, M.C., *History of Modern Indonesia Since c. 1300*, (Second Edition), London : The Macmillan Press LTD 1993.

Rodwell, J.M., *The Koran*, (trans.) London : Everyman 1992.

Rose, Gregory F., "Shi'i Islam: Bonydgiri or Fundamentalism," in Sahliyeh, Emile, *Religious Resurgence and Politics in the Contemporary World*, New York : State University of New York 1990.

Rosidi, Ayip. *Beberapa Mas'alah Umat Islam di Indonesia*. Bandung : Bulan Sabit 1970.

Runciman, W.G., *Relative Devripation and Social Justice*, Berkeley : University of California Press 1966.

Sahliyeh, Emile, (ed.), *Religious Resurgence and Politics in The Third World*, New York : State University of New York Press 1990.

Samson, Allan, Islam and Politics in Indonesia, PhD dissertation, University of California, Berkeley, 1972.

Sanad, Jamal and Tessler, Mark, "Women and Religion in a Modern Islamic Society," in Sahliyeh, Emile (ed.), *Religious Resurgence and Politics in The Contemporary World*, New York , 1990.

Sarwono, Sarlito W., *Perbedaan Antara Pemimpin dan Aktivis dalam Gerakan Protes Mahasiswa*, Jakarta : Bulan Bintang 1978.

Schwarz, Adam, *A Nation in Waiting: Indonesia in the 1990s*, Sydney : Allen and Unwin 1994.

Shireen, T. Hunter (ed). 1988. *The Politics of Islamic Revivalism: Diversity and Unity*. Indianapolis : Indiana University Press.

Shupe, Anson, "The Stubborn Persistence of Religion in the Global Arena," in Emile, Sahliyeh, *Religious Resurgence and Politics in the Contemporary World*, New York , 1990.

Siddiqui, Kalim, *The Islamic Movement: A Systems Approach*, London : The Open Press Limited 1980.

Siddiqui, Kalim, (ed.), *Issues in the Islamic Movement: 1983–1984 (1403–04)*. London : Open Press 1986.

Smith, Charlotte Seymour, *MacMillan Dictionary of Anthropology*, London : The Macmillan Press LTD 1986.

Suminto, H. Aqib. *Politik Islam Pemerintah Hindia Belanda*. Jakarta : LP3ES, 1985.

Tamara, M. Nasir. *Indonesia in The Wake of Islam*. Kuala Lumpur : ISIS 1986.

Tapol. *Indonesia: Muslims on Trial*. London : Tapol The Indonesian Human Rights Campaign, 1987.

Tehranian, Madjid, "Islamic Fundamentalism in Iran and the Discourse of Development," in Martin Marty, E. and Scott Appleby, R. (eds.), *Fundamentalism and Society: Reclaiming the Sciences, the Family and Education*. Chicago : The University of Chicago Press 1993.

Turner, Bryan S., *Orientalism, Postmodernism and Globalism*, London : Routledge 1994.

Vatikiotis, Michael R.J., *Indonesian Politics Under Suharto: Order, Development and Pressure for Change*, (New Updated), London : Routledge 1994.

Voll, John O., "Renewal and Reform in Islamic History: Tajdid and Islah," in Esposito, John L. (ed.), *Voices of Resurgent Islam*, New York : Oxford University Press 1983.

Wallace, Athony F.C. 1966. *Religion An Anthropological View*. New York : Random House.

Wallace, Anthony F.C., "Revitalization Movement," in Lessa, William A. and Vogt, Evon Z., *Reader in Comparative Religion, An Anthropological Approach*. New York : Harper Collin Publishers 1979.

Ward, K.E. *The Foundation of the Partai Muslimin Indoensia*. Ithaca : MIP Cornell University, 1970.

Weber, Max, *The Theory of Social and Economic Organisation*. New York : Oxford University Press 1947.

Wetheim, W.F., 'Indonesian Muslims under Sukarno and Suharto: Majority and Minority mentality', in Hering, B. (ed.) *Kabar Seberang Sulating Maphilindo*, Townsville : James Cook University of North Quennsland 1986.

Wetheim, W.F., *Indonesian Society in Transition: A Study of Social Change*, Bandung : Sumur Bandung 1956.

Yaqzhan, Muhammad, *Anatomi Budak Kuffar Dalam Perspektif Al-Qur'an: Telaah Kritis Fenomena Perbudakan Pemikiran Gerakan Pembaruan Keagamaan (GPK) di Indonesia*, A-Ghirah Press.

Zuhri, K.H., Saifuddin, *Sejarah Kebangkitan Islam dan Perkembangannya di Indonesia*, Bandung : Alma'arif, 1981.

Articles, Papers, Documents

Ahmad, Leila, "The Resurgence of Islam : The Return to the Source," *Histoty Today*, 30, February 1980, 23–27.

Bahasoan, Awad, "The Islamic Reform Movement: an Interpretation and Criticism," in *Prisma*, Vol.35, March 1985, 131–60.

BKPMI, *Sekilas Tentang Badan Komunikasi Pemuda Masjid Indonesia (BKPMI)*, Jakarta : BKPMI.

Dahlan, Mursalin, *Latar Belakang Pemikran Ide Pendirian LP3K* (Unpublished Paper), 1994.

DKM STTM, *Forum Silaturahami Lembaga Dakawah Kampus se-Bandung Raya dan Priangan Timur IX*, Bandung : Dewan Keluraga Masjid Sekolah Tinggi Teknologi Mandala, 1994.

Drakeley, Steven, "Islam in Indonesian Politics," *Current AffairsBulletin*, July 1992, 4–12.

Enayat, Hamid, "The Resurgence of Islam : the Background," *History Today*, 30, February, 1980, 16–22.

FSLDK, *Sejarah Perkembangan Forum Silatrurrahim Lembaga Dakwah Kampus*, unpublished paper.

Hefner, Robert, W., "Islam, State, and Civil Society: ICMI and The Struggle for Indonesian Middle Class", *Indonesia*. No.56, October 1993.

Hopper, E. and Weyman, A., "Modes of Conformity and Forms of Instrumental Adjustment to Feelings of Relative Devripation," in *British Journal of Sociology*, Vol.27, 1975, Pp.66–77.

Kantor Sensus dan Statistik Kotamadya Daerah Tingkat II Bandung. *Sensus Penduduk 1980, Rekapitulasi Kotamadya Bandung* (Unpublished), 1980.

Karisma, *Sejarah Singkat Karisma*, (Unpublished paper).

Kuntowijoyo, "Islam as an Idea," *Prisma*, No. 35 Mrach 1985.

Lyon, Margo, L., "The Dakwah Movement in Malaysia," in *Review of Indonesian and Malayan Affairs*, 13:2, 1979 (34–45).

Moghadam, Valentine, M., "Rhetorics and Rights of Identity in aislamist Movements," *Journal of World History*, Vol.3 No. 1 Soring, 1992.

Perwataatmadja, Karnaen, A., "Menyambut PT Asuransi Takaful Keluarga", *Republika*, 26 August 1994.

Pipes, Daniel, "'This World is Political!!' The Islamic Revival of The Seventies," *Orbis*, Spring 1980, 9–41.

PPM Fi Zhilal, al-Qur'an, *Obsesi Melahirkan Generasi Qur'ani yang Unik (Al-Jail al-Farid)*, Bandung : Yayasan Fi Zhilal al-Qur'an, 1991.

Rais, Amin, "International Islamic Movements and Their Influence Upon the Islamic Movement in Indonesia," *Prisma*, No.35 March 1985.

Rakhmat, Jalaluddin, "Islamic Fundamentalism: Myth or Reality," *Prisma*, No 35, March 1985.

Regan, Daniel, "Islamic Resurgence: Characteristics, Causes, Consequences and Implications" *Journal of Political and Military Sociology*, vol. 21 no. 2 Winter 1993.

Risnawati, "H Abdullah Gimnastiar Ngimpi Kasumpingan Nabi Nagdegkeun Bengkel Akhlak Daarut Tauhid," in *Mangle*, No. 1431, 15 December 1993.

Smith, T.M. and Carpenter, H.F., "Indonesia University Students and Their Career Aspirations," in *Asian Survey* ???Septembet, 1974, Pp. 807–28.

Tholkhah, Imam, *Bahasa, Budaya dan Kekuasaan dalam Pandangan Anderson*, (Unpublished paper), August 1994.

Wright, Robin, "The Islamic Resurgence: A New Phase?," *Current History*, 87, 526, February 1988, 52–6.

Yayasan Istiqamah, *Laporan Umum Musyawarah Kerja Paripurna Pengurus Lengkap Yayasan Istiqamah tanggal 6 Februari 1994.* (unpublished paper).

Newspapers and Periodicals

Antara, 26 October 1992.

Far Eastern Economic Review, 24 January 1985, 26–31.

Far Eastern Economic Review, 11 August 1994.

Forum Keadilan, No.5, 23 June 1994.

Futures, Vol. 23 No.3 April, 1991 (Whole issue)

Hidup, No 7, 12 February 1989.

Hidup, Nop.13, 26 March 1989.

Inside Indonesia, No. 8 October 1986, p. 3.

Kompas, 3 September 1991

Mizan, Vol.3, No.2, 1990, 49–53.

Muslimedia, November 1983.

Panji Masyarakat, No. 365. 11 June 1982.

Panji Masyarakat, No. 469. 1 June 1985.

Panji Masyarakat, No. 529. 1 February 1987.

Panji Masyarakat, No. 621. 21 August 1989.

Panji Masyarakat, No. 623. 11 September 1989.

Panji Masyarakat, No. 628. 1 November 1989.

Panji Masyarakat, No. 629. 11 November 1989.

Panji Masyarakat, No. 630. 30 November 1989.

Panji Masyarakat, No. 632, 11 December 1989.

Panji Masyarakat, No. 633, 21 December 1989.

Panji Masyarakat, No. 649. 1 June 1990.

Panji Masyarakat, No. 650. 11 June 1990

Panji Masyarakat, No. 650, 11 June 1990.

Panji Masyarakat, No. 664, 1 November 1990.

Panji Masyarakat, No. 665, 11 November 1990

Panji Masyarakat, No. 669, 21 December 1990

Panji Masyarakat, No. 676, 11 March 1991

Panji Masyarakat, No. 734, 11 October 1992.

Panji Masyarakat, No. 758, 11 June 1993.

Panji Masyarakat, No. 774, 21 November, 1993

Panji Masyarakat, No. 784, 1 March 1994.

Panji Masyarakat, No 798, 21 July 1994.

Panji Masyarakat, No. 799, 10 August 1994.

Panji Masyarakat, No. 808, 1 November 1994.

Pelita, 4 December 1990

Pelita, 26 April 1991

Pelita, 6 December 1991

Pelita, 13 March 1992

Pelita, 23 May 1992

Pelita, 18 August 1992

Serial Media Dakwah, February 1989.

Serial Media Dakwah, March 1989

Serial Media Dakwah, April 1989.

Serial Media Dakwah, August 1989.

Suara Pembaruan, 7 December 1990.

Suara Karya, 3 June 1992.

Suara Karya, 7 December 1992.

Suara Merdeka, 13 December 1991.

Tapol, 92, April 1989.

Tempo. 8 September 1979.

Tempo, 27 February 1982.

Tempo, 29 December 1984.

Tempo, 9 May 1987.

Tempo, 14 June 1986.

Tempo, 18 February 1989.

Tempo, 13 May 1989.

Tempo, 27 October 1990

Tempo, 3 November 1990.

Tempo, 8 December 1990.

Tempo, 3 October 1992

Tempo, 3 April 1993

Tempo, 4 September 1993.

Tempo, 20 November 1993.

Tempo, 4 December 1993.

Tomtowi Syafei, 2, September-October, 1987.

Ulumul Qur'an, No 3 Vol.IV 1993, Whole issue.

Ulumul Qur'an, No 2 Vol. V, 1994, 86–95